Faith, Family and Fighter Jets

From his action-packed sequences in the clouds to his down-to-earth conversations and humorous moments with his children, Todd Riddle gives you an authentic look at the real life and faith of a fighter pilot who loves God, loves his family, and loves his military career. His biblical encouragement, practical applications, and gut-level transparency will inspire you to integrate your faith into your family and work life too, so God can be glorified, and you can experience a life well lived.

—**Cindi McMenamin**, national conference speaker, Bible teacher,
pastor's wife, and author of seventeen books, including
When Women Walk Alone, When God Sees Your Tears, and
When Couples Walk Together (coauthored with her husband, Hugh)

Faith, Family and Fighter Jets is the ultimate dad book! It has the adrenaline of a fighter pilot, the tender love of a father, and the practical parenting tips of a great teacher. I was gripped from beginning to end with Colonel Todd's life, and it made me want to be a better dad. The "Riddler" skillfully uses his tactical military training to help us become better parents. Each chapter is gripping, manly, humble, and very accessible. *Faith, Family and Fighter Jets* slayed me. I'm a believer in this book.

—**Mark Foreman**, lead pastor at North Coast Calvary Chapel,
author of *Wholly Jesus* and *Never Say No: Raising Big-Picture Kids*

Colonel Todd "Riddler" Riddle takes the readers on a twisted and hilarious journey into his life as a decorated A-10 fighter pilot and laughably a failing children's sports coach. Riddler expresses his story in a way that captures the hearts of believers and those who want a relationship with Christ, while straying away from the traditional and predictable stories to meet readers where they are on their spiritual journey. *Faith, Family and Fighter Jets* is a great and entertaining must read.

—**Chad Robichaux**, author of *An Unfair Advantage, Fight for Us,*
Behind the Lines, The Truth about PTSD, and *Path to Resiliency*

In his book *Faith, Family and Fighter Jets*, Todd the Riddler has done a great job of bringing together the challenges of life as a fighter pilot with the challenges of everyday living. His candid approach clearly connects with highly confident folks like us fighter pilots—especially the male ones who are quick thinkers and slow learners in relationships. His stories can help us all learn and grow. So kick the tires and light the fires and start turning those pages.

—**Leon "Lee" Ellis**, CSP, Colonel USAF (Ret.),
and president of Leadership Freedom LLC

Even if you've never served in the military or experienced combat, you will relate to Colonel Todd Riddle's stories of courage in the face of adversity and trusting the Lord amid life's trials. *Faith, Family and Fighter Jets* will encourage you!

—**Jim Daly**, president, Focus on the Family

Colonel Todd Riddle has written an amazing look at the airman experience that couches an inspirational and introspective guide to a fulfilled and spirit-driven life. Riddle provides levity and guidance from his experiences inside and outside of a fighter jet. He displays a warm and infectious personality, an unwavering positiveness, and a down-to-earth demeanor that allows him to connect and share experiences with anyone. *Faith, Family and Fighter Jets* is an accessible guide to finding faith and inspiration in any situation.

—**Scott Smith**, professor of marketing,
University of Central Missouri, Warrensburg, Missouri

Todd Riddle has lived a very interesting and challenging life as his book *Faith, Family and Fighter Jets* shows. It is always refreshing to hear how someone in a hazardous profession implements his Christian faith as he lives his life.

—**Tom Osborne**, College Football Hall of Fame,
National Champion coach, and former US congressman

Not only do I want to become a fighter pilot and grow an obnoxiously elaborate mustache, but more importantly, I want to create "radical fans" in my life. Colonel Todd Riddle in his book *Faith, Family and Fighter Jets* has provided great insight on how I can transition radical fans for me to radical fans for Jesus.

—**Jay Rapley** MD, orthopedic sports medicine surgeon,
Rockhill orthopedic specialist

A lifelong family friend, I met Colonel Todd "Riddler" Riddle when he was sixteen years old and playing smashmouth football under the Friday night Nebraska skyline. His tenacity enabled him to overcome obstacles on the gridiron and propelled him to a life of valiant military service to our nation. Be inspired by Colonel Riddle's courageous leadership as he invites you to discover the time-tested principles of faith, family, and freedom in his book *Faith, Family and Fighter Jets*.

—**Karen Bowling**, executive director, Nebraska Family Alliance

In his book *Faith, Family and Fighter Jets*, Colonel Todd "Riddler" Riddle combines compelling detail with introspection and even humor as he takes readers from the intensity of flying an A-10 fighter jet in a combat mission, to the antics of a college student fleeing the scene of a prank, to the tender reminiscence of a football coach dad who gained insight from the players he guided. Brilliantly written, this inspiring book provides usable advice for leaders and encouragement for us all.

—**Tammy Real-McKeighan**, news editor and faith columnist, *Fremont Tribune*, Nebraska, and author of *Spiritual Spinach: Faith for the Journey*

SHACK! Riddler is right on target in inspiring and motivating people to examine the most important things in their life and how to impact those around them. Wherever you are in life, *Faith, Family and Fighter Jets* is the perfect wingman to guide you to greater fulfillment and achieving a grander purpose.

—**Lietunent Colonel Kenyatta "Deacon" Ruffin**,
US Air Force fighter pilot and White House Fellow

Todd Riddle's *Faith, Family and Fighter Jets* will inspire you, fuel your faith, change your perspective, and give you insights on how to live out God's destiny for your life. My friend Todd's passion for God, zest for life, unquenchable hope, and steadfast faith will ignite a spark in you to live life to the fullest and change your world.

—**Pastor Solomon Wang**, vice president, Convoy of Hope

With brutal honesty, humor, and great storytelling, Colonel Todd Riddle in his book *Faith, Family and Fighter Jets* invites us into the cockpit of his fighter jet to experience hair-raising encounters that forged the grit and grace needed for success, not only on the battlefield but also in navigating everyday life. His ability to translate lessons learned in combat to the boardroom, classroom, and family room makes this book essential for readers looking to elevate the significance of their relationships and service to others. Grounded in the timeless truths found in Scripture, this book will have you on the edge of your seat in suspense on one page and laughing out loud on the next.

—**Mark Balschweid**, professor and department head of Agricultural Leadership, Education, and Communication, University of Nebraska-Lincoln; senior fellow of the American Association for Agricultural Education

In this book *Faith, Family and Fighter Jets*, Colonel Todd Riddle paints stunning visual pictures of life for the reader as he shares his story as a fighter pilot and how God has used it in his journey to be more like Jesus. We are entertained by his honest and at times self-deprecating stories while in the air and at home. The similes he brings from his time in combat bring valued and practical insights for all. And his intriguing and humorous stories from his life as a fighter pilot translate to real-life leadership principles for any follower of Jesus. He is a humble warrior bearing his soul to us and in turn challenging us to see our own stories as part of something grander.

—**Rick Lorimer**, lead pastor, Christ Place

If you want a mix of real-world action, whimsey, provocative questions, engaging stories, and serious reflection, then *Faith, Family and Fighter Jets* is for you. If you want candor touched with humility, this book is for you. Todd Riddle's fighter-pilot experience, painted in detail, is a lens through which we can see ourselves and our lives in a fresh way. I reflect on writing most often with one question: "What did I learn in that reading?" The answer here is, "Things I can engage and practice this very day!" Thanks, Colonel Riddle, for telling us your story and defending our freedoms.

—**Dick Foth**, coauthor of *Known: Finding Deep Friendships*
in a Shallow World

You had better get to the ER if your pulse doesn't increase after reading Colonel Todd Riddle's story of supporting US ground troops in the Afghanistan mountains while flying through a hail storm! In *Faith, Family and Figher Jets*, Todd's wonderful gift of telling his authentic story with humor and a ton of heart and then connecting that story to God's mercy and grace is nothing short of remarkable. His love for Jesus, his dear family, and his country will continue to inspire me to "put on love" when I wake up each morning.

—**David W. Anderson**, PhD, founder of Impacting People,
and cohost of the *Red Truck Marriage* podcast

With his genuine integrity, love for his family, dedication to his country, and commitment to his Christian faith, Todd Riddle and his family impressed me from our first meeting. His wisdom shaped my own leadership skills in those areas. And his insight compels me to pursue deeper relationships and to fight for all that is good and right and true in this world.

—**Chad Puckett**, executive director, Show-Me Christian Youth Homes

Wow! *Faith, Family and Fighter Jets* is a great and easy ready that is entwined with the grace and mercy of an almighty God who sees the vulnerability of a man's life journey with him. To hear about Colonel Riddle's tight spaces in battle and practice and some of the choices he made while as a fighter pilot for our great nation is as real as it gets. Add to that the glimpses he gives us into his life as a boy and young man and to becoming a father and we have in these pages a great example of what we need today. Great job, Colonel Riddle!

—**A. J. Nunez**, pastor, Covenant Worship Center, Fresno, California, and executive director, Mighty Men Movement

In his book *Faith, Family and Fighter Jets*, Colonel Riddle doesn't hold back. He shows you what he has seen. You are there with him as he learns. He's not afraid to share his mistakes. You feel the weight of the jet and get a clear view of wisdom well earned.

—**Mark Oh**, MD, emergency medicine, southern California

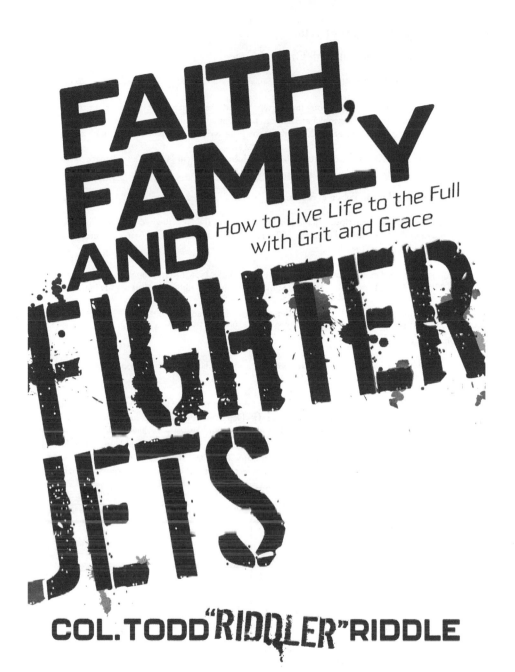

FAITH, FAMILY AND FIGHTER JETS

How to Live Life to the Full with Grit and Grace

COL. TODD "RIDDLER" RIDDLE

NASHVILLE

NEW YORK • LONDON • MELBOURNE • VANCOUVER

Faith, Family and Fighter Jets
How to Live Life to the Full with Grit and Grace

Published in New York, New York, by Morgan James Publishing. Morgan James is a trademark of Morgan James, LLC. www.MorganJamesPublishing.com

Proudly distributed by Ingram Publisher Services.

Unless indicated otherwise, all Scripture quotations are taken from the New Revised Standard Version, Updated Edition. Copyright © 2021 National Council of Churches of Christ in the United States of America. Used by permission. All rights reserved worldwide.

Scripture quotations marked NIV are taken from The Holy Bible, New International Version® NIV® copyright © 1973, 1978, 1984, 2011 by Biblica, Inc.™ Used by permission. All rights reserved worldwide.

Scripture quotations marked NASB are taken from the New American Standard Bible® (NASB), copyright © 1960, 1962, 1963, 1968, 1971, 1972, 1973, 1975, 1977, 1995, 2020 by The Lockman Foundation. Used by permission. www.Lockman.org.

Scripture quotations marked NKJV are taken from the New King James Version®. Copyright © 1982 by Thomas Nelson. Used by permission. All rights reserved.

The opinions expressed in *Faith, Family and Fighter Jets* are strictly those of the author alone and do not imply or constitute endorsement by the US Air Force, US Department of Defense, or any part of the US government. Thank you to the Defense Office of Prepublication and Security Review for their clearance of this manuscript without alteration for open publication reference 21-SB-0113. Personally Identifiable Information of all individuals have been protected in this manuscript or with expressed written consent. This work depicts actual events in the life of the author as truthfully as recollection permits and/or can be verified by research.

Morgan James BOGO™

A **FREE** ebook edition is available for you or a friend with the purchase of this print book.

CLEARLY SIGN YOUR NAME ABOVE

Instructions to claim your free ebook edition:
1. Visit MorganJamesBOGO.com
2. Sign your name CLEARLY in the space above
3. Complete the form and submit a photo of this entire page
4. You or your friend can download the ebook to your preferred device

ISBN 9781631958830 paperback
ISBN 9781631958847 ebook
Library of Congress Control Number: 2022930980

Cover Design by:
Rachel Lopez
www.r2cdesign.com

Cover Photo by:
Neil Dunridge
Instagram: @ndunridge

Interior Design by:
Christopher Kirk
www.GFSstudio.com

Morgan James is a proud partner of Habitat for Humanity Peninsula and Greater Williamsburg. Partners in building since 2006.

Get involved today! Visit MorganJamesPublishing.com/giving-back

*To Sarah, whose zeal for the Lord and free laughter make all
of this flying and praying and working have purpose.
You make our life together a delight and are the picture of grit and grace.*

*From Sarah, who dedicates this book to fellow souls
who have lived with a fighter pilot!*

CONTENTS

FOREWORD

I believe that *Faith, Family and Fighter Jets* is the single most important book to come out of America's longest war—the war on terrorism. Here's why.

Evil is the absence of love, just as darkness is the absence of light. And God defeats evil with love. Love for our families, love for our nation, and (most importantly) love for our God are among the weapons that a loving God uses to fight evil in this world. And this is a book about a man who fiercely loves his family, his nation, and his God.

In the aftermath of the terrorist attacks in America on September 11, 2001, Americans such as Todd Riddle have been hunting down the forces of evil across the globe.

Evil. What else do you call it when terrorists fly planes full of helpless men, women, and children into buildings in order to murder those passengers and thousands of others like them in those buildings?

Evil. What else can you call it when our enemy beheads helpless bound victims and then proudly disseminates the video recording of these horrific acts around the world?

Evil. What else do you call it when terrorists burn an enemy pilot alive in a cage? This is what terrorists did to a Jordanian Royal Air Force pilot who was shot down and captured.

Add to such atrocities the many beheadings of other captured enemy combatants and civilians that some of our enemies have conducted, video recorded, and posted on the internet and even used to recruit others to their side. What else would call these acts other than evil?

Colonel Todd Riddle and the American pilots who have flown with him would have been treated just as badly if they had ever been shot down and captured by the enemy in this war. So when Colonel Riddle's son turns in a school project entitled "My Daddy Kills Bad Guys" (see chapter 20), we need to recognize the simple wisdom and truth spoken by a child.

As a Christian, I know that Jesus died for terrorists every bit as much as he died for you and me. God loves them, so we who follow him try to respond to them with love. Instead of beheading captured terrorists or burning them alive, we strive to treat them with dignity and respect. Rather than intentionally seeking the mass murder of innocents, we have fought a war with the lowest levels of collateral damage ever seen in modern times, often placing our own troops in danger rather than accepting possible harm to innocent civilians. That is how we fight evil with love. We "do not repay evil with evil" (1 Peter 3:9 NIV). While a soldier must shoot and possibly kill an enemy, as soon as the enemy is captured or has surrendered, the soldier will call the medic to save the life of the person who tried to kill them. In each case, they are practicing what Paul says love does: "[Love] always protects" (1 Corinthians 13:7 NIV).

With the US withdrawal from Afghanistan in 2021, that part of the war may have come to a conclusion but the global war on terrorism continues, and US armed forces must still go in harm's way around the world. Colonel Todd Riddle is one of these warriors. He is among the many men and women who fight by night and day, in distant lands, across the globe, defeating evil with love. As is so very well said by Riddle:

> One reason fighter pilots win is that, when called to fight, we rise to the occasion and boldly run toward the sound of the guns. Not in a twisted view of bloodthirst, but as a very human response to the nature

of God imprinted on our lives. There is no greater love than to place ourselves in harm's way, potentially to die, for another.

Throughout this war, our citizens have thanked our warriors, but the truth is that our military men and women volunteered for this; they were not drafted. And they take great satisfaction in what they do. Here's Riddle again:

> I have been fortunate to experience many highlights, and I expect your stories, which I hope this book have triggered, reflect the handwriting of a loving God through each retelling. Epic events are great to reflect upon, and they help urge us along when the path gets lonely or difficult. I have been fortunate to fly into sunrises and sunsets over the Atlantic and the Pacific, to have dogfought F-18s from Finland, to have landed at places that aren't officially places, to have parachuted with green berets, to have flown faster than the speed of sound, to have killed bad guys and helped rescue some good guys. I've seen my three children born, coached Little League, swam with sharks, stayed in a fourteenth-century castle with my wife, and raced an Audi A-6 on the Autobahn in Germany. I have briefed senators, met an ambassador, tactfully disagreed with four-star generals, been hugged by an Afghan warlord, floored the accelerator on a Ferrari, and chased giraffes from a jeep in Kenya. . . . [But] All of these things are meaningless garbage if they cost me my faith and relationship with those I love. . . .
>
> I fly jets to go to war and protect American lives and kill bad guys because it's what I feel called and motivated to do. You don't have to thank me for that.

The military families are the real heroes of these decades of war, and they most deserve our thanks. Colonel Riddle shows us how they, too, are motivated by love:

I have witnessed my kind and diminutive wife boldly wade right into the middle of the lives of single moms and paroled dads whose history of drugs, jail, and bad choices dared to compromise the future and safety of their precious kids. She pours out her life, her treasure, her time and heart with no promise of a return on the investment. Brushing right past her own fears, heartaches, and uncertainties, she remains unwilling to defer to someone "better" who has yet to show up.

Thus, a loving God has raised up a new Greatest Generation forged in decades of war.

I began to humbly understand that there is not a place that our Creator will not go, a darkness, history, or desperation that his presence and orchestration cannot conquer. Perhaps the inky black fingers of despair grip at each of us at times, "the night holds onto us" as a song lyric calls out. Still, the assurance exists that, when inviting an eternal God into our lives, the darkness no longer has any power over the light. With reliance on him and in cooperation with him, we can become beacons of light that will draw others through dark times.

Faith, Family and Fighter Jets is the best book today that continues the narrative of faith, service, and sacrifice exemplified by so many warriors and their families. This is a living, faith-filled resource from and for a new Greatest Generation empowered by God's love as they fight an epic battle against forces of evil. This book informs, inspires, and calls us to good, godly greatness. It is a pathfinding, trailblazing book, showing us how to balance God, family, and service. And not just military service. You'll find in this book practical counsel for service in business, in our families and churches, and even to ourselves as we seek to love others as we love ourselves (Matthew 22:39). Love is all-encompassing, covering every aspect of life, and Todd Riddle knows this.

He also is not hung up on himself. He tells hilarious stories, often at his own expense, and he uses even these to show us how we can learn to humbly love others *and* act with courage, sacrifice, and perseverance no matter the vocation we have been called to embrace.

I encourage you not to just read this book but to also study it and strive to apply it to your own life. May it be a mighty blessing upon you, your family, your church, and your nation.

Lt. Col. Dave Grossman (US Army, ret.)
Author of *On Killing, On Combat, On Spiritual Combat, Assassination Generation,* and *Sheepdogs: Meet Our Nation's Warriors* children's book

1

WHAT THE HAIL?

"Faithful trumps successful."
—Brad Riddle

The jet slowly rumbled along the runway, gaining speed and groaning a bit under the weight of bombs, bullets, and rockets. I pulled back slightly on the stick, setting the nose to a few degrees above the horizon while letting the jet accelerate a bit more before getting airborne. I've always preferred a bit more "smash" (airspeed) when the jet feels a little sluggish and I'm flying within the mountain bowl and thinner air at Bagram Air Base in Afghanistan. There were beautiful, towering white clouds rolling over the base and toward the Hindu Kush mountain ranges northeast of our position toward the Kunar province. It was 2008, and I was grateful and energized to be flying the Hawg again, ready to punish the deserving enemies of our nation and proud to be a member of the 303rd Fighter Squadron—the "World's Greatest Fighter Squadron. Seriously." At least that was our toast in the bar.

Weather conditions made it impossible for us to get to our assigned airspace, so we flew using an instrument approach back to Bagram to get below the clouds. Flying south of Bagram and now below the weather, we received an urgent radio call directing us to immediately proceed to an area east of Gardez, near the Pakistan border. The chattering radios told us to rush to support a crippled US convoy that had struck an improvised explosive device (IED). As we raced toward the friendly troops, intercepted enemy radio calls were relayed to us and indicated a second impending attack of more than a hundred terrorists. After moving the refueling tanker closer to our convoy and topping off with fuel, I headed toward the convoy as my flight lead then swapped roles and headed for the tanker (called yo-yo operations). I strained to understand the ground controller (known as a JTAC, Joint Terminal Air Controller) on the radio as the mountain valleys and frequent pops of lightning affected our communication. He was separated from the convoy by another mountain valley a few miles to his east as he tried to relay to me what was happening. I skirted alongside some dark clouds, just above the mountains, trying to make sense of where the good guys and bad guys were. The truth was, the guys on the ground weren't sure where the enemy was, and in the low ground along a river gorge, they were frightened knowing that they had just survived an explosion, had vehicles they could no longer drive, and were expecting a follow-on attack.

Sliding along the periphery of the storm, which looked to be building in intensity, I found the friendly location on my map display. The US soldiers were in a narrow river gorge that was about four hundred meters across and surrounded by vertical rock faces 13,000 feet high. I had entered and exited the weather looking for a clear avenue of approach. Unfortunate luck had the friendly convoy perfectly centered beneath the building storm. I was hoping to find some clear air and quickly locate the friendlies and terrify the enemy into inaction before killing them. An air-to-ground strafe with the indescribable GAU-8 Avenger 30mm Gatling gun on which I sat was the most incredibly accurate, rapid, and effective of weapons. The terrorists of Afghanistan knew the lethality of the A-10 well. Radio intercepts overheard them calling the Hawg the "Monster" and imploring one another to remain in hiding until our presence was thought to be gone.

Realizing I was going to have to fly directly into the storm to get to the convoy, which could get a little ugly, I made a quick radio call to confirm our troops weren't simply hoping for an airshow or a "morale pass." The strained voice of the JTAC and what I could overhear of the convoy coming through the radio made me a little embarrassed to ask. He requested an immediate show of force. A show of force lacks the Hollywood-like opportunities to provide "kinetic effects" (code words for blowing stuff up) but is often used as a rapid deterrent to enemy forces and a critical reassurance to our vulnerable soldiers on the ground of the mighty A-10's presence and protection. It can also buy some time and protection during a hostile situation to sort out locations and target sets and to arrange a quick game plan. As a rule, fighter pilots would rather shoot the enemy than scare them, but inherent to our training is to do the best we can with whatever pitch is thrown.

So I tried to hit the pitch as hard as I could. I turned the jet east and flew into the storm, heading for the friendlies and the river gorge. The jet began to bounce quite a bit with turbulence and heavy rain. Very quickly the entire cockpit got dark as I was enveloped by angry clouds. I had checked the altitude on my map that would keep me safe above the mountaintops: 13,300 feet was the number. The turbulence grew more intense, and the jet was pitching up and down 1,500 feet. I noticed I was continuing to climb higher into the weather with each of my corrections, reducing the likelihood that I might be able to see the ground and provide help. I've heard other pilots call this the "I want to live" instinct. Usually a good instinct, it wasn't helping me as I continued to pull the jet higher in an overcorrection to get back to altitude. My profane self-corrections were later heard on my mission tape and laughed about at a fighter pilot roll call. I had forgotten to turn off my hot microphone after refueling so each breath and mumbled word were recorded.

A few miles from the friendlies, hail started hitting the jet. It became deafeningly and surpisingly loud as hailstones the size of tennis balls peppered Tail #093. After all, I was in a closed cockpit, wearing a helmet with ear cups and foam ear protection. Still, the roar of hail hitting the jet at 300 miles an hour was startling. I kept banking the jet up to try to see some sliver of ground that I could dive toward. A hailstone then hit the canopy with incredible force and cracked the outer layer of bulletproof glass. As I was directly over the top of the friendlies, I turned north to follow the mapped path of the river gorge to try to find an opening. A thin green ribbon of agricultural fields along either side of the snow melt river suddenly appeared. As I rolled the jet on its back to dive beneath the weather, a second hailstone struck the front glass, again cracking the canopy. It felt like getting hit by a steel shot put thrown at 300 miles per hour. I rolled the jet on its back and dove toward the river gorge. Clear now of the hail and heaviest rain, the jet passed 375 knots and raced toward 400 knots. For an A-10 airfoil that isn't exactly svelte, these airspeeds generate an uptick in parasitic drag causing the jet to become nosier. I remember pulling the throttles back a little bit—a negative habit transfer from our high-altitude dive-bombing techniques. This was a mistake as I would need every knot in a few moments. I screamed past the convoy, dispensing flares, banking the jet up in their direction, hoping to present the visual and audible threat to the gathering enemy.

Straining to find the friendlies, I was quickly past them and needed to immediately begin an aggressive climb back into the weather as I had reached the end of the canyon. At 45 degrees nose high and nearly entering the weather again, a final hailstone struck the canopy while the thunderous noise of other hailstones striking the wings, slats, tail, and engine nacelles began again. Entering the dark clouds, I followed my displayed position on the moving map as I tried to calculate if I could make a safe altitude before running out of room. I wasn't sure I trusted my own mental math (known as "gonk" to flyers), trying to calculate altitude gain versus airspeed loss before I ran out of room. My quick gonk seemed to be cutting things too close, or maybe I was just a wimp. I zoomed in on the map scale to find which direction the river turned at the south end of the gorge. I was trying to follow a lower minimum safe altitude a bit longer as my jet continued a labored climb.

Moments later, I flew out of the southwestern side of the storm into blue sky. I checked out the condition of my jet, looking as though it had suffered a terrible back-alley beating while the engines still flawlessly hummed along. I wanted to puke in my mask. In my haste, I had forgotten to close the precious targeting pod (another mistake), and the leading edges of the jet were pocketed with dents and missing paint. The ground troops and JTAC, now emboldened and moments later assured that the attack had been dissuaded, thanked me over the radio and were able to safely leave ("egress") the area without attack.

I radioed ahead my emergency status while internally second guessing my decisions. I assured all listeners that the jet was flyable, the engines were sound, and that Tail #093 would not fly again for awhile. The aircraft flew flawlessly, the landing was uneventful, and I was fortunate to navigate around the armada of fire trucks with red lights flashing in case I needed help. I taxied my battered but unbowed Hawg back to the ramp to park. A large audience of pilots, maintainers,[1] and the wing commander watched me park and shut down. I could read the lips of our maintenance chief master sergeant as I turned the last corner and he saw what I brought home. More profanity. Waiting for me at the bottom of my ladder and looking like a father ready to confront a teenager for missing curfew was the wing commander. He had quickly earned a reputation for grounding pilots. Climbing down the ladder, I nervously announced to him and the small greeting party of fellow leaders that "I've got full coverage insurance with GEICO, and I'll pay the deductible." The snorted laugh of a squadron leader broke the tension, at least my tension. The wing commander didn't laugh. Perhaps my comedic timing was poor.

Arriving to work the next day after a long night of tape review, writing a narrative statement, and having a physical exam and blood drawn following my "mishap," my squadron commander told me he was "trying to get you back flying as quick as possible." I took this to mean that I was grounded pending an investigation.

Hail damage is not considered a combat related loss so I spent the next few days completing additional narratives, signing documents of disclosure, and testifying to two separate safety boards, one in Afghanistan and another back in Louisiana via video-teleconference. Had the jet been full of bullet holes, there would have been fewer questions. But flying into an embedded thunderstorm did not fit any combat damage definitions regardless of the circumstances. Now under a requisite safety investigation, several layers of scrutiny regarding my flying preparation, competence, judgment, training, sleep cycle, and diet were now under review. With the sleepless self-examination that followed, I began to wonder if or when I would be allowed to fly again, if there would be some embarrassing disciplinary action that would keep me out of the cockpit or forever label my career.

Although unnerving to be so closely examined, my team of leaders were clearly and selflessly in my corner immediately. The A-10 maintenance community was incredibly supportive of what I had done and demonstrably proud of how well their aircraft performed under the extreme conditions. My group commander, an incredible A-10 warrior-leader, strongly defended my actions when the wing commander told him that the A-10 guys needed to "back-down a little bit." The response that came back was "We don't back down. Ever." What a great quote; the kind you would expect from a Hawg guy, a former NCAA Division-1 hockey player, and eventual brigadier general. An investigating pilot from the F-15E community also sought me out to compliment my efforts after reviewing my mission tape.

My reaction in 2008, as well as my reaction today, is mixed. I did the right thing and performed at a high level, though not with perfection, when it mattered the most. I made mistakes in my efforts, but, more significantly to how I process success or failure, I didn't have the satisfaction on this occasion of employing weapons, seeing the explosions, and knowing with certainty that my actions made a difference. The safety board presiding officer's comments and the after-action report noted my actions as commendable while simultaneously the wing commander's brief grounding of me carried its own ambiguity and stigma.

Success, or my romanticized visions of success, would have involved multiple strafing gun runs on our enemies followed by a reunion with the endangered troops complete with cigars, shared laughter at another near-death experience, and a renewed sense of commitment and belonging to our own band of brothers. But the real-world script on this day didn't resolve so clearly, and I grappled to understand how success seemed cruelly indifferent to being faithful. Success, whether seen through our lens or the romantic camera lens of Hollywood, has clear, predictable, and highly preferred outcomes. Faithful service requires a higher calling to duty that can immediately do the right and courageous thing to the best of one's ability, with no wasted energy or loss of focus lamenting the circumstances, opportunity, and even need for resolution.

Whether flying, coaching, or spousing, I am called to be faithful to the truth and love of Christ and his lordship in my life. However faithful the steps, knowing and doing what is right and noble may not always be synonymous with our cultural definitions of success. Faithful works are guided by principle and a love for others, not driven by calculated outcomes or economic returns on investment. Faith-driven decisions are not to be understood as a license to be foolish, rather they are an acknowledgment that God's sovereign economy follows different rules and places different values on life than does a standard business balance sheet. In the eyes of those who only see numbers, status, or advancement as success, faith and duty may seem foolish at worst or charitable at best.

The great British political leader William Wilberforce was credited with abolishing slavery in England and all its territories after thirty-seven years of exhausting parliamentary failures and infrequent, partial successes. He embodied a life ransomed to a faithful pursuit of the right thing even in the face of professional, financial, and physical ruin. Success can be elusive, arbitrary, or even disputed. While abolition was always the goal, Wilberforce followed a life calling, a high and noble purpose, that refused to be slowed by the obstacles and discouragements of what his peers would qualify as serial failures.[2] But serial failures, when read as chapters of the larger story, demonstrate that God remains sovereign even amid ambiguity.

Aware of my very human limitations to understanding, while also making room for a sovereign Creator to be at work in our world and lives, cues me to know that ambiguity will always exist on this side of heaven. And we are encouraged to make room for and lean in, with trust in the Lord, to fill in the gaps of our understanding, efforts, and plans, all the while depending on his active role in our lives. "Trust in the LORD with all your heart and lean not on your own understanding; in all your ways submit to him, and he will make your paths straight" (Proverbs 3:5–6 NIV).

My hope and passion are twofold:

- That our character matures to that of a Wilberforce, that even our impromptu choices flow from a deep commitment to eternal biblical truths—truths that I have been taught and seen lived out while working around the world with fighter pilots. These are universal truths that should compel each of us, regardless of our vocation, to love others and act with courage, sacrifice, and perseverance.
- That we would resolve and be driven to remain faithful to the right things over that which is popular or convenient or may meet a fleeting template of "success." Our challenge is to embrace the call to obedience and service like Wilberforce did, to walk potentially difficult paths. Wilberforce committed himself to the right thing, even in the face of decades of mockery and few successes, to die only three days after slavery was finally abolished. While Wilberforce is an exceptional example, we can each at least aspire to seasons of faithfulness to the right things when others may misperceive our efforts as failing.

Dick Foth is a pastor I appreciate. He recalled in a message his days as a young church intern for his father-in-law. Dick commented on the seemingly unlimited willingness of a parishioner to volunteer substantial hours to help. Dick's father-in-law warned: "Be careful, Dick. He'll do anything you ask as long as you throw him a parade." If the success were to dry up, if the parades and notoriety were to stop, or if things were to become difficult, there wasn't a confidence that the volunteer had steeled in his heart to genuine service or a truth he held dear over the common and vain need for recognition.

Inevitably, the lines of our pursuits between faithful works in small matters and direct pursuits of success might blur. At times I wonder, am I cognizant of doing the right thing, even in small matters, as a preeminent matter of character building, or only if I might be thrown a parade? Our hope should be that faithful works will bear fruit in our character to eventually fill the most lasting measures of success in this age and the age to come.

We all seem to struggle with and encounter those individuals who must always match another's exploits, or one-up them in the telling. This is affectionately known as "mad dogging" in my fighter squadron, named after a known offender. As my pastor has said, it's better with such people to "let 'em go and run out with the line." That is, resist the urge to perpetually try to compare or compete to feel more significant and successful. A faithful pursuit can be encouraged by appropriate recognition, but our efforts to support the right thing ought to present without a parade.

I was returned to flying duty a few days after the hailstorm. Returning home a few months later, an article appeared with pictures of my battered A-10 to commend aircraft maintenance and myself. I received a safety award, the irony of which did not escape the squadron. "How can you get an award for recovering from an emergency you caused?" I was asked. The question came loudly from the back of a laughing public forum. A valid point I noted and without my dispute. I kept the award anyway. Future grandchildren won't need to be bothered by that part of the story. Our wing commander also pointed me out during a crowded squadron roll call and loudly announced that "Someone should have given Riddler a medal instead of grounding him!" Friend and fellow fighter pilot Dozer quipped, "Can't *you* give medals, colonel?"

Relying on others, including leaders, to label our efforts as "successful" can be inconsistent or unsatisfying and may too fully empower others to dictate our own sense of worth and direction. We must embrace some element of grace to know that, in a fleeting moment of decision making and without a Hollywood scripted ending, ambiguity may be the dominant label for our actions, and our lone consolation is the knowledge that we did the best we could. We can't choose the era in which we are born nor author every circumstance under which we live, study, work, and perform.

I couldn't choreograph a perfect tactical situation and outcome for the hailstorm day. I, like each of you, cannot control the pitch that is thrown. All I can do is determine, regardless of circumstance and perhaps plagued with uncertainty, that I am going to hit the pitch I get thrown as hard as I possibly can and do something, such as fly into a hailstorm, approach a stranger in need, invite a struggling friend to lunch, mentor a neglected youth, or buy a single mom a washer and dryer. These are ways to hit the pitches thrown to us and to choose being faithful over self regard and success. Swinging at a pitch only when perfectly scripted outcomes are possible is no way to fly a fighter jet and not a way to live our lives. We must hope to live with such character and calling that we might endure thirty-seven Wilberforce years of faithful character building before arriving at the desired and fullness of success. We may even change our world as result.

THUNDERBOLT TAKEAWAYS

Here are some key mission de-brief points for each of us to consider:

- ✗ Success can be elusive, fickle, and subjective.
- ✗ Duty is demanding.
- ✗ Divine sovereignty triumphs over ambiguity.
- ✗ Grounding our life in biblical truths anchors us during difficult seasons of confusion and shifting norms of moral or vocational expectations.
- ✗ The well-being of others may often trump our own comfort, certainty, and affirmation.
- ✗ Criticism and scrutiny will always travel with changemakers.

Life is messy, and our questions do not always find resolution. But as we understand that God calls us to be faithful and that we are not called to a modern image of success, we can swing the bat without hesitation and lean on our heavenly Judge to relay understanding and our life score. Little else really matters. The apostle Paul was right when he exclaimed: "Yet whatever gains I had, these I have come to regard as loss because of Christ. More than that, I regard everything as loss because of the surpassing value of knowing Christ Jesus my Lord. For his sake I have suffered the loss of all things, and I regard these as rubbish, in order that I may gain Christ" (Philippians 3:7–9).

The A-10 is an amazing jet with an amazing community of professional maintainers. This photo shows what my aircraft looked like after the hail-storm; this is the leading edge slat of the left wing. The engines never even hiccuped! I flew the same jet, #093, with my name on it for years afterward.

This is looking down on the cracked canopy. I am standing at the left in the picture, holding a flag flown in the cockpit on the sortie, explaining my comprehensive coverage insurance plan to my leadership. After which I was briefly grounded.

2
SATCHEL'S STOOL

"I now see that I spent most of my life in doing neither what I ought nor what I liked."[3]
—C. S. Lewis

Hall of Fame baseball pitcher Satchel Paige lived an extraordinary life, reflective of his unique athletic talents and a folksy wisdom that helped him survive a challenging life start. The lens through which he viewed life was unique to his athletic talents and highly personalized views on work, contentment, and keeping a youthful spirit. While known to have lived his life to excesses, I have also found his assortment of insights from life to pitching to be uniquely simple and insightful. Satchel would have done well in our evolving work-from-home culture because there was no difference in his public or private persona. Satchel understood a holistic way of integrating each area of his life, communicating an authenticity and vulnerability that drew others to him.

There is a quote, often attributed to him, that addresses three critical pillars of our lives. These pillars and our ability to balance and connect their interaction with a healthy life really define who we are as people and how we relate to others. Much like Satchel's life, the quote is also not without mystery, dispute, and a handful of claims concerning its origin—an origin attributed to a number of sources, including ancient Irish proverbs, an American folk singer, writer Mark Twain, and particularly disgruntled lyricists Susanna Clark and Richard Leigh. Here is the counsel:

> Work like you don't need the money.
> Love like you've never been hurt.
> And dance like nobody is watching.[4]

At a minimum, Satchel's life and his collection of quotes embody the spirit of these pillars of our lives and provide a good framework for us to evaluate our own well-being and those near to us. With credit to the Irish, lyricists Susanna and Richard, Satchel, and a folk musician, the balance of our own lives, the three-legged stool on which our values interconnect, consist of our work, our relationships, and whom we love as well as what brings us joy and a sense of contentment. Perhaps the universality of the insights also makes accurate attribution more difficult.

My father-in-law was raised on a farm in northern Nebraska, and as is typical of that generation and geography, was milking cows before dawn at four years old. My friend, Les, was also a dairy farmer and explained to me why a milking stool has three legs. With three legs instead of four, the three-legged stool is the most stable platform on which you can sit that can rest on uneven ground and be less likely to wobble. Designed to be stable while placed on the uneven ground of a milking barn or field, it is always possible to draw a plane through three points. The angle might not be ideal, meaning you might slide off, but it is the best design to get a usable sitting platform before tucking it underneath a cow and putting your hands places I don't want to touch.

Likewise, there are underlying values that drive our decisions and behaviors in each of the "legs" of our lives. Also, each of these legs, for the stool to have any utility, must emanate from the same point. The stool doesn't work very well if there isn't a seat at the top. In the same way, for our stool of life to be stable and useful on uneven ground, each unique leg—our work, our relationships, and our contentment—must extend from values that are consistent through every area of our lives. For our lives to have coherent meaning, our faith or moral code and commitment to universal ideals, such as truth, perseverance, forgiveness, nobility, and sacrifice, must remain steadfast as inevitable challenges and differing interpretations will occur.

As we explore the work areas of our life, regardless of vocation (and yes, stay-at-home parent, volunteer, or retired greeter at the state park all classify as work), current books implore us to find our strengths as well as why we do what we've chosen to do. With respect to those questions, nurturing the attributes of what we love most into our daily efforts can help to center our why amid endless tasks. While we need money to function, my kids tend to prefer food with their meals, and contentment rests upon those able to value their own purposeful productivity above a number on a paycheck.

Crises, pandemics, and deathbed encounters have the power to immediately bring into focus what may have been previously fuzzy in our eyes—eyes that had become fixated on the monotony and tumult of each day. I have never heard of a deathbed confession whereby someone said, "I wish I had stayed later at the office" or "I regret all of those family picnics." Relationships are the most powerful area of our lives, able to compel great emotions of affection or laughter and yes, even pain. We are not designed to live in isolation. Nurturing the relationship leg of our stool—in other words, striving for high quality connections with others—is the most rewarding and potentially challenging area of our lives.

On each of my five deployments and on twenty-four years of lengthy training trips away from home, I continue to be surprised at how quickly I can miss things that I had come to expect or take for granted only a few weeks before: a bucket of golf balls or cold morning surf before work, a funny movie with my family, a motorcycle commute through the state park where I can clearly hear the exhaust rumble loudly off the trees. Making room to cherish fun, joy, and relaxation helps to enliven and season every area of our lives. Healthy pleasure helps to lift the heaviness of life's burdens and heartaches while restoring and refreshing us to be sharper for the next challenge and for those who need us to be at our best.

Life inevitably provides an unstable, ever-changing base for Satchel's three-legged stool. On occasion, the *work* leg will become too dominant, traumatizing the *relationship* leg and causing us to neglect the *dance* leg. Seasons of life will cause these three elements to continually shift in proportion to one another. The challenge is not to maintain this stool in some utopian perpetual balance but to courageously grapple with the unending fine-tuning of each of these three areas of our lives. A healthy interwoven or balanced view of these areas does not mean equal in time or money but a tuned balance for our own well-being and functionality. To continually neglect and avoid the imbalances we encounter results in unhealthy repercussions. As seasons of our lives, age, workplace, and children's development stages change, so do the opportunities to adjust how we need to resettle the stool on shifting ground.

THUNDERBOLT TAKEAWAYS

- ✗ Well-being requires a commitment to the holistic weave of physical, emotional, mental, and spiritual health.
- ✗ Healthy resilience aims higher than simply being able to absorb the blows of life. It keeps us grounded when circumstances seem overwhelming, and it enables us to thrive and move forward when our very instinct invites us to retreat and take cover.
- ✗ Balanced living requires a dynamic cross-check of our work, relationships, and contentment that adjusts our nurturing to the areas of our lives that are most important to our health, not simply the most respondent to the needs of the day.

Hall of Fame pitcher Satchel Paige in action.
(Used by permission and with thanks to the Negro
Leagues Baseball Museum, Kansas City, MO)

3

THE WILD WEST

"Does your mom know you're here?"
—MSgt. Robert Boye, A-10 crew chief

s of this writing, I'm in my mid forties and have posters of Captain America and life-size stickers of the 1979 Dallas Cowboys' players on my walls. As a kid, on Halloween I wore various homemade superhero costumes complete with a red dish towel for my cape or a sword cut out of cardboard and covered with aluminum foil. Backyard football games included my own version of loudly delivered radio commentary to detail game-winning plays. I knew very early in life that I would never be the strong safety for the Dallas Cowboys or realize the athletic stardom of those on the posters on my walls, but that didn't keep me from admiring these men.

My parents adhered to the free-range parenting of the 1970s that allowed you to wander the town until street lights came on, drink from the garden hose, watch cartoons, build ramps for your bike, and by extension, imagine and chase your dreams. Those childhood dreams for me held the great appeal of danger and adventure, justice and nobility, and competition and teamwork. Family picture albums show me standing with my hands on my hips outfitted in Captain America Underoos. A bright-eyed expression says I hadn't learned yet to doubt myself, be practical, or have any concern with what others thought.

I enjoy asking audiences what they dressed up as for Halloween. What did they dream of being when they grew up? Some jump right in and are animated in their recollections. One woman loudly told our group of seventy-five that she dressed up as a Dallas Cowboys cheerleader and wore her mom's "stripper boots." The class boomed with laughter, and other members couldn't share their childhood whimsy fast enough.

The best bosses to work for, the most compelling employees to have, and the most intriguing leaders are those able to embrace the whimsy and curiosity of life that seems to bring them more alive and more fruitfully chasing a grander vision than the rest of us. Nurturing whimsy and curiosity, desires for growth, and the aspirations of dreams are often born in little hearts and represent a noble purpose.

I attempt to approach my roles as husband, father, leader, and follower with those unabashed and youthful ambitions. Wanting to honor the legacy and faith of my parents, unleashing my children or subordinates to dream, and helping create an opportunity to compete or chase after what awakens them form a roadmap for a life of purpose and strength. Such a roadmap provides a reference and a direction to run amid the inevitable detours and hardships that mark our journey.

Realizing the Dallas Cowboys were never going to call my name on draft day and that Captain America had been injected with a super serum not yet available to the public, I discovered a job that seemed to combine the best of what I loved. I picked a path that made me come alive. I became a fighter pilot. My job is to pull the trigger on an aircraft called an A-10C Thunderbolt II.

Mr. Engle was my eccentric seventh grade English teacher. He gave us an assignment to send a letter to any school or college we chose and ask for more information. We had to use strange implements, like pencils and stamps. As I read through the list of schools, the United States Air Force Academy sounded a lot cooler than my local college. I had already decided that I wanted to fly jets, and it seemed the Academy was the way to do it. It was the only school to which I applied during my high school years. While my teachers told my parents during conferences that I was only in school for the sports, I managed to nurse a GPA high enough to give me a chance to fly jets someday. I had always loved sports, but my goal to get into the Academy and fly drove every other extracurricular activity. ACT tutoring from a teammate, study habits, and even a family vacation for my parents to see what this Academy thing was about helped me go after a dream.

The path from my seventh grade letter to becoming a qualified combat-ready fighter pilot was not a straight path. In fact, I had no idea of the steps, roads, efforts, and obstacles that would come between me and a cockpit. Refusing to hear no is a common personality trait of those whose roadmap is a fighter cockpit. For instance, shortly after arriving at the Academy, cadets and parents were notified of profound cuts to pilot training slots following the post Desert Storm drawdown in the 1990s. With a shoulder that kept dislocating during basic training and watching upper classmen leave the school, my wandering route commenced as I left the school and assumed that a childhood dream must not be in the cards. Frankly, doing something else seemed easier. Nevertheless, following two shoulder reconstruction surgeries, another air force scholarship opportunity that failed to align, a broken arm, continued cuts to military pilot slots, a flunked depth perception test, a delayed and precarious medical waiver, and a college transcript that read like a "choose your own adventure," I finally had an opportunity to fly. I just took the long way around to get there.

I arrived at Bagram Airbase in Afghanistan in May of 2002 as a combat mission-ready A-10 fighter pilot. This was two years after my first military flight, and a lifetime removed from the 1986 English letter-writing assignment. Bagram was a former Russian airfield in a dusty bowl beneath sheer rock mountains. I was quickly amazed by the Wild West environment as Bagram had been unattended for decades, and abandoned Russian fighter jets called Migs that I had only seen in grainy black-and-white pictures were piled up at the ends of the airfield. The noise and silt combined into a loud swirl in my eyes, nose, and food as my every step sunk to my ankle in the moon dust under my feet. I slept in a tent that had a floor built of cargo pallets. As the newest and youngest arrival, my pallet and cot were near the front tent flap. The pallet beneath me was also inconveniently balanced on a large rock that moved the cot and myself up and down several inches each time someone stepped into the tent. Our showers were in a bombed out Russian building, the wall frames of which were constructed partly of empty ammunition cans. There was only one complete wall, which consisted of some plywood, and a blue tarp for a roof. A garden hose on a hook and the plywood provided some separation from the filth. The improvised floor had a 10-degree downslope toward the wall, both of which were covered with black mold. As I stood naked under the stars, trying to get clean for a few moments, my shower shoes slid on the slick film on the floor toward the moldy wall. I stuck out one finger to hold my position away from the plywood as I choked back my gag reflex.

Mealtime was also a full contact experience as strong winds tore apart the dining tent, threw plates in the air, and mixed dirt into our food. The dirt did provide some seasoning. At my first meal, I watched a Russian-made helicopter land a few hundred yards away, not something I had ever seen before. The pilot walked to the tent and sat across from me. He was dressed in civilian attire, had long curly black hair, was wearing a gold bracelet, and was armed with a Russian machine gun. In a measure of childlike faith, I convinced myself that he must be a good guy if they let him on base. I didn't attempt any small talk. A friend remarked that our lunch table, with the number of special forces, bounty hunters, and other government agency personnel sitting at it, "looked like the bar scene out of *Star Wars*."

A few days after my arrival, I was scheduled for my first ever combat sortie with a weapons officer named Hut. As we drove to the jet, I thought of many of the same things other fighter pilots think: *God, don't let me screw this up; I don't want to let the other guys down; It's about time, a chance to play for real and kill some bad guys.* I also had some satisfaction that after years of dreams, hard work, detours, and doubts, I had finally made it! As I walked to the jet across a dilapidated apron of concrete with piles of dirt shoved out of the way, recently dug drainage trenches, and sun-splashed mountain ranges in the background, my chest swelled with a sense of pride and satisfaction.

Wearing a G-suit and carrying a helmet and other flight gear, I took off my sunglasses to shake the hand of Bob, a seasoned crew chief standing next to my assigned mighty A-10 Warthog. Looking down on me, the crew chief studied my fresh face and "new kid" demeanor for a moment. Smirking at what he saw he asked, "Does your mom know you're here?" Poor Bob didn't seem to care how monumental this moment was for me.

The jet was a little heavy for the takeoff conditions of summer heat and higher elevation. Our takeoff involved a significant amount of planning as various runway holes had been marked by cones and sandbags. The east half of the runway was closed a few thousand feet down where a six-foot-deep trench was being filled and rebuilt by an Italian civilian engineering crew. After I ran up the power and watched Hut's jet waddle down the runway, I followed his lead, tracking an initial slalom course around various holes from the right side of the runway over to the left and back to the right. As I straightened out and accelerated for takeoff, I noticed the runway repair crew lined up down the closed side of the runway, just on their side of the cones and in front of the trench. They were all bent over with their hands on their knees. And as my jet accelerated past them, they waved like a crowd at a football game. This was the Wild West.

After a first combat sortie of armed convoy escort, reconnaissance, and area orientation, some fellow pilots met me at the jet to congratulate me. In the weeks ahead, we would regularly return from a sortie to our homemade three-sided plywood "Officer's Club" for Cuban cigars and an episode of *Band of Brothers* with our squadron mates.

While savoring the idea that dreams come true, there was an early wake up the next morning, new intelligence reports to review, a new weapons load to calculate, and jets that needed our attention. A sixteen-year goal became a great photo and a great memory among a career treasure trove of similarly amazing "I can't believe we just did that" moments. For me, flying a combat sortie in a single-seat jet was a great milestone.

Milestones are markers for life's journey, not exit signs designed for us to pull off the road and take up permanent residence at a rest stop. My favorite football coach, Hall of Famer and former US Congressman Tom Osborne, has spoken about how satisfying national championships are in realizing decades long goals. But he speaks more fondly of cherishing the journey and the process of pursuing those goals.

> With God removed from the equation, I have found life to be devoid of real meaning. You simply can't win enough games to satisfy yourself or others. No matter what your profession is, there are always some accomplishments that exceed your grasp. . . . I've always enjoyed the relationships with the players and coaches more than the trappings of success. . . . The real secret of enjoying sports is to focus more on the process than the scoreboard.[5]

The relationships, the obstacles overcome, and doing life with others are viewed as the more rewarding experiences. After all, those national champion coaches wake up the morning after a game and, while the coffee may taste better, they are on the road recruiting that same day, taking the next step of the process, persevering through hardship with a grit that is able to endure—and doing all with a sense of purpose and a dream of the next great thing.

As a dad, I want to extend the legacy of my parents to my children, to live equal parts of the paradox that invites whimsy and imagination as well as the necessary grit to fuel oneself through the inevitable hardships that find all of us. I remember a story (maybe a fable) of a seasoned fighter pilot who agreed to fly a jet back to his hometown for an airshow and a recruiting opportunity. As the sun was setting, he noticed a boy had been watching him from the fence. As the pilot walked past, the young boy said, "Mister, when I grow up, I want to be a fighter pilot." Wryly, the pilot smiled and said, "Son, you can't do both." The amount of laughter, hijinks, and banter that happens at a deafening level in the hallways of my flying squadron attests to another quote from Satchel Paige: "How old would you be if you didn't know how old you were?" Unlike pants that get too small or have grown out of fashion or a VCR that is long since obsolete, it is never too late to have a fresh dream, a vision of growth, or simply the delight of pursuing what makes you come alive.

Whether a change of direction amid a wildly successful position, moving on from frustration, or simply working to tweak your present role, cultivating those attributes that most bring you alive is critical for tapping into your reservoir of energy and ideas. Growth is always a possibility whether we're talking about a first job or a late retirement hobby or anything inbetween. Your ability to contribute on this planet is not done. As speaker and legislator Les Brown says, "You are never too old to set a new goal or dream a new dream."[6] Too many options can paralyze us to remaining in park. Here's a bump for you from timeless questions to get you moving and to help narrow your search for what you might excel at or be energized by next:

- Do you prefer focusing on people or tasks?
- Does your natural disposition maintain a quick or methodical pace?
- Do you enjoy being creative or novel with few restrictions, or do you take a sense of satisfaction from repeatable and precise problem-solving?
- What comes easily to you that is difficult for others?
- What subjects might you be able to discuss that leave you feeling more energized than fatigued?

These questions might sound familiar to students who take high school vocation tests. A mere awareness of how to discover where you are at your best, by itself, doesn't mean you are actually pursuing opportunities to be at your best. Perhaps another place to start is to recall what you dressed up for on Halloween. What pictures did you have on your walls as a child? What activities or imaginations brought you the most delight as a ten-year-old kid? These may hold more of a key to your future than you might imagine.

THUNDERBOLT TAKEAWAYS

Modern writers encourage us to be purpose-driven, to find our why and be a part of something larger than ourselves. Pursuing the desires of our heart with a purpose in eternity is the backbone of the biblical roadmap we find. The wise author of Ecclesiastes encourages us that "Whatever your hand finds to do, do it with all your might" (Ecclesiastes 9:10 NIV). I like the freedom we have in Christ to choose *whatever* we want, presuming we've committed our work and talents to honor him.

I remember grappling through my late teens and early twenties with discovering what I thought must be a singular occupation or vocation that God had willed for my life. A pastor later encouraged me to realize that God's will is more like a playground. Pick what you want, with obvious room for the wisdom of family or friends and your own history of performance, but pick what you want. We simply need to remain on the playground that embraces our vocation as but one area of our lives in which faith has been allowed to flood and saturate every room and chamber of our hearts. John Eldredge in his book *Wild at Heart* shares a great quote, the kind of quote that can immediately reorder how we individually understand purpose, meaning, and the value of our work: "Don't ask yourself what the world needs. Ask yourself what makes you come alive, and go do that, because what the world needs is people who have come alive."[7]

✔ Confidently trust that what dwells in your heart has originated from a godly design.

Equally important to finding what on the playground enlivens us is to sift those dreams and interests to find what is worthy of further investigation and pursuit. "Take delight in the LORD, and he will give you the desires of your heart" (Psalm 37:4) is not a magic genie passage that presumes that, with an active faith, I will be rewarded with whatever I want. Rather, as my heart becomes more Christlike, I will submit my desires, hopes, and dreams to our Creator who will then redeem and refine them for opportunities to fulfill them. Equally whimsical is the thought that while serving an eternal God who has infinite creativity, we might also birth new interests and visions through various seasons of life that he is able to enrich and purify. Life can truly be an adventure with God!

✔ Dreams die without effort and grit.

Dreams without work, risk, and sacrifice fail to become purpose-driven visions and instead become fantasies of Neverland with little value and real-world impact. Amid an entire culture in which all suffering or hardship is vigorously removed or avoided, a great parenting tragedy is to model for our children and orchestrate their development in a way that always finds the path of least resistance. Then we help nurture an entire generation of human beings who never learn anything of failure or experience surprise at their own reservoir of strength to persevere.

Our culture suffers from an absence of grit. A study of over 11,200 West Point military academy cadets over the course of a decade found that grit was the single greatest predictor of graduation success over that of physical or cognitive abilities. A University of Pennsylvania study by Dr. Angela Duckworth et al. defined grit as "passion and perseverance for long-term goals of personal significance." More significant than the best brains and brawn of some of our nation's most elite students is the ability of those who have the strength of ambition to push onward when the road ahead might become dim, littered with obstacles, or take an unexpected turn. Duckworth and her team summarize, "Talent isn't enough; sustained and focused application of that talent is what truly matters."[8]

Satchel encouraged us to "work like we don't need the money" long before the research of billion-dollar organizations and capable authors today urge us to have meaning and be socially responsible. Perhaps Satchel's ideas are simple by comparison. But for our vitality and an enduring legacy for those we share life with, the ability to blend the whimsy and imagination of dreams that transform us and our world with the grit to persevere through hardship and obstacles are the best formula for realizing a life that might surprise us and cause others to ask, "Does your mom know you're here?"

Flight line at Bagram Air Base, Afghanistan, 2002;
the "KC" tailflash and associated National Football League
Kansas City Chief's Arrowhead logo belong to the
303rd Fighter Squadron, Whiteman AFB, MO

My first career combat sortie with "Hut" as part of the reknowned 75th Fighter
Squadron Tiger Sharks, Bagram Air Base, Afghanistan, 2002

Bagram's first Officer's Club in June 2002, the predecessor to the "Billy" now featured at Pima Air Museum. A three-sided plywood lean-to named 17 India after an airspace designation where the initial Operation Enduring Freedom sorties were often assigned.

4

WHAT ABOUT LOVE?

A war-weary President Lincoln, with lines deeply etched in his face carved by both his personal losses and the unrelenting weight of the blood and death paid to preserve the Union, was asked how he would treat the rebellious South shortly following General Lee's surrender. Lincoln's eternally wise and unpopular response was to endeavor to treat the South *as though they had never rebelled*. Unfortunately, that did not become policy or law. As brilliantly detailed in Ron Chernow's book *Grant*, postwar atrocities continued as the Union lurched forward and back in a struggle to reintegrate the South. The ramifications of this attempt still reverberate today. But we know from the nation's highest leader, the commander in chief of the

armed forces, that President Lincoln desired a restoration that required a measure of forgiveness that seemed too lenient to the victorious North. He intimately understood that unity required a reverence for others and a decision
to forgive and press forward together even when emotions and the counsel of
others advocated for harsh punishment.

Relationships provide an intimacy of spirit and deep connection with those
in our lives and are the richest measure of our own health, well-being, and
sense of belonging. Our Creator's design from the very beginning realizes that
we are not meant to live in isolation. Soon after creating Adam, "The LORD
God said, 'It is not good for the man to be alone. I will make a helper suitable
for him' " (Genesis 2:18 NIV). The Author of life tells us that it's not good
for us to be alone. We each need a tribe to be a member of, an intimate circle
of friends or family who know our every fault yet cherish us and insist on
counting us as one of their own. Heritage, legacy, purpose, and sacrifice are all
values that intersect in our hearts between us and those we love.

Satchel's folksy wisdom speaks to a core issue of the relationships in our
lives. To say "Love like you've never been hurt" presumes we will all be hurt
at some point. Relationships, interpersonal communication, and just plain life
are messy sometimes. We will become wounded, angered, wronged, or simply
misunderstood. And along with being hurt, we will cause hurt to others as an
inevitable outcome of our frail human condition. The depth and frequency of
these hardships are as unique to each of us as fingerprints.

While emotional wounds might be the horrible intent of someone with a
black heart or a result of illness or dysfunction or simply careless words or
selfishness, forgiveness is critical to living in committed and healthy relationships. Whether in big ways or small, being able to extend, request, and receive
forgiveness is a hallmark of relationships that are valued and resilient. True
love is not fragile, and one way it expresses itself is through forgiveness.

Now forgiveness does not imply some blind tolerance of abuse or patterns
of dysfunction or negligence. Rather, an identifying challenge that follows true
forgiveness is to determine if we are waiting for an apology. If we are, then we
likely don't fully understand forgivness.

My wife and family know firsthand my own frailty. I get impatient when I'm tired, and I become frustrated when rules or bureaucratic processes impede my "grand vision" for more efficient shortcuts to the results I value. I tend to align with the camp of those who think rules often exist for people who can't think on their own. My wife, however, thinks rules exist to protect society from, well, people like me. My personal triggers get energized by a few things, and the obvious result is, I'm not at my best. I have become accustomed to apologizing, asking for forgiveness, and attempting to change habits that can be harmful. In twenty-six years with my wife, her extension of grace, her forgiveness, and acceptance of the hard parts of having a relationship have shaped our marriage, my leadership, and how I understand what forgiveness means.

Grace or mercy can be difficult for us to grasp, and it is difficult for us to humbly ask for forgiveness and admit fault. It may be even more difficult to surrender our rights to be angry at an offense and to try to move forward while wounded and extend grace and forgiveness to another. We may need to change the nature of a relationship. Perhaps more intimacy or time for space may follow depending on the nature of the wound. Forgiveness doesn't mean that we are always obligated to restore all things as though we're not changed by our experiences. We may, in fact, need to revise healthy boundaries. Still, forgiveness does ask us to cherish relationships enough to potentially experience some pain amid the growth of committed and resilient connections with others.

Living in the Midwest, our family has made the most of the Ozark Mountains, the Great Lakes, and, Branson, Missouri. We enjoy the limestone hills, Table Rock Lake, the folksy restaurants, great golf courses, and kind people. Branson is a veteran friendly town, and, inevitably, we're at a show where veterans are asked to stand when their service song is played. My family elbows me in the ribs, and I stand up. The other attendees look at us gratefully and imagine the patriotic sacrifices many have made in countless deployments and in austere conditions under hostile fire or rocket attack. Amid those noble warriors, I want to tell those people that I fly jets to go to war and protect American lives and kill bad guys because it's what I feel called and motivated to do. You don't have to thank me for that.

Probably like most of you, I don't prefer being away from family and have missed dozens of birthdays, holidays, special school programs, reunions, and preschool graduations, but the combat is why I do my job. The more personally painful patriotic sacrifices happen while still in the United States, with family an arm's length away, on a Saturday in the fall with a clear blue sky. College football is on TV, my family is at home eating something with cheese on it while I sit in a chemical mask and charcoal protective suit hollering into a radio preparing for a pretend Russian attack—all the while in Missouri. I am not belittling the rigors of combat or the criticality of training; training for combat is relevant and necessary. But missing a Saturday with family for pretend war ranks way up there on my list of annoyances or sacrifices I make to get to fly jets. And in light of the real sacrifices made by so many others, it's an annoyance that really isn't all that noteworthy.

In a two-year training cycle, we were preparing for an Operational Readiness Inspection in which we surge how many total sorties we can fly, test our ability to load bombs and guns, execute personnel and medical processing, repair runways, and all amid persistent simulated chemical or rocket and missile attacks. I was assigned to work as an operations liaison to our maintenance team during these training exercises. Affectionately my job was called the "Rat," and working side by side with my maintenance partners for those years, I became somewhat of a midget pilot mascot who worked hard to blend the flying needs and maintenance capabilities amid stressful circumstances. One Saturday I sat pouting in my work truck, smelling badly, as did my sweating partners wedged in there, with a buckle on my gas mask jamming into my head. I had missed countless days of flying because of this task over the last year, my Huskers were airing on TV, we seemed stalled on how we were improving in the exercises, and, importantly, I didn't remember the movie *Top Gun*, which first dropped the dream of flying jets into my heart in a small three-screen local theater in 1986; I never saw any make-believe war scenes with pilots wearing a charcoal-filled coat while sitting in a truck.

Suddenly, the windsock on top of a nearby hanger swung wildly the other direction and the sky darkened. Within minutes we were in a full crisis recalling jets from all directions and attempting to get as many aircraft safely hangered as possible.

As the wind and debris swept across the flight line, radios crackled with urgent directions, and I felt something hit the back of the truck. I turned around but didn't see anything. Then I could hear and feel something. Thump, thump, thump—it bounced along my side of the truck. Then, in a surreal dreamlike scene, a blue portable toilet bolted on plastic skids floated off the side of the van and slid in front of the windshield. Pausing a moment, it was caught again by another gust of wind resulting in a smooth half pirouette and pivot in the direction of the jets.

Taking a few moments to process what we were seeing, with mouths agape, we watched as a blue box of poop seemed to smoothly accelerate away from us while heading for the jet parking spots. Cackling with laughter at the absurdity, we jumped from the truck and chased down the potential weapon of mass destruction. After seizing the offending Porta-John, we weren't sure what to do next. A young airman of only one stripe had bounced to our aid and suggested we could "tip it over so it won't blow away." Tip it over? A Porta-John? There was a reason that kid only had one stripe. We weren't going to tip it over. We wedged the blue box between some generators and opened the door to let the guy out who was stuck in there (I made up that part).

I learned so much from those years of close quarters work with the great A-10 maintainers. And perhaps the laughter of that day, the strange combination of sharing both the best and worst of experiences, carried us forward for remaining untold hours of chemical masks and rubber overboots.

To cherish relationships is to value not only those to whom you are related or married or obligated. Treasuring others is to move beyond simply surviving work together or being cordial and professional. Relationships are the most soulful and spiritual leg of our stool. We are hardwired to feel connected to others, to have a tribe in which we "do life together." The flying box of poop accelerated that connection in a way that digital connections or shared videos of cats can never replace.

Families bond in a very similar way. No one in my family calls each other by their given names. Maybe your family is the same way. My father, Dr.

Brad Riddle, is known as Papa Howie. My mom is Crazy Grandma Judy. My brother, Dr. Eric Riddle, is known as Fast Ed, and my sister, Bethany, is Squirrely. We started calling my brother Fast Ed based on his initials and an awkward pulpit introduction from a pastor over thirty years ago. I'm affectionately called Chuck by family members or Charles on formal occasions. I honestly have no idea why "Chuck." I think it may have something to do with a bad haircut and Chuck Taylor Converse shoes. Some stories are better off lost to time. Silly names, of course, but shared history and the embrace of those who have celebrated with us in our best moments and supported us in our worst are how we make room for love in our hearts and how we communicate that "You are one of us. We know you, and, for better or worse, you are connected to us, and you have a place."

As a nonflying and begrudged pilot during the inspection exercises, of course I was too shortsighted to realize how my maintenance coworkers, who truly became partners and friends, would shape my leadership and build a trust that enabled our unit to develop some unique and demanding capabilities in the years to follow. Sharing successes and failures and witnessing each other's strengths and weaknesses under hardship removed any superficial veneer that could cloud our communication or veil our true goals. That honesty and trusted partnership did not happen in the first months of our training. Learning the maintenance vocabulary and priorities, being transparent and consistent in what precisely the flying operation needed, including mistakes we may have been making, built a credible bridge with those working so hard to get the jets in the air. Over the next ten years and as the deployed commander, the foundation of that trust allowed a simple arrangement. I understood the maintainers' mission enough to be confident in their substantial capacity, while also being careful not to ask for something impossible or beyond what was truly necessary. Their leadership trusted me enough that when I did come asking for something big and I was willing to "own the risk" of that request, they wouldn't tell me no. Negotiation was inevitable but not antagonistic as we were ultimately pulling toward a common goal, only modifying the specifics and turnpoints of how we were to accomplish the steps on the way.

My kids have recently complained that I never lose an argument. Crazy Grandma Judy has said the same about Papa Howie, and my wife has said the same about me. My fighter pilot instinct, akin to that of an eighth grader, wants to respond, "Learn to argue better and maybe you'll fight to a draw," followed quickly by "Pull my finger." Gratefully, my higher angels do exist, even if muted, and convict my heart to realize there must be some pride or arrogance hurting the relationship leg of my stool. I have character flaws that sometimes make it difficult for my loved ones to speak out of their hearts freely or to disagree with me. I don't want my individual idea of balance upset, but that can also adversely affect the interconnectedness of my stool. A loving character that honors relationships requires us to be approachable, regardless of whether we are likely to agree. As a dad, I acknowledge that I am not 100 percent correct all the time, so why do I still find myself positioning to win? Additionally, am I, by default, modeling behavior to my kids that I am unapproachable and too proud to be conciliatory or empathic? I think my loved ones are less concerned with winning than being heard and understood.

Good leaders maintain an emotional intelligence that is mature enough to no longer feel a need to be the smartest person in the room, the most witty, or to win every exchange. The advantage of my experience as the "Rat" was that it was obvious to me and everyone else that I had no idea what I was doing and was completely in learning/receiving mode. Being receptive to instruction inherently communicates a humble spirit that allows others to be the authority. It also builds trust by valuing others and nurturing a cooperative spirit. Aspiring pilots, some I have taught, found themselves out of flying or saw their career take a sharp turn for the worse when their rigidity or insecure nature caused them to continue to fail to be receptive to instruction. There can be harsh consequences, both personally and professionally, for failing to completely own and respond to weaknesses, flaws, or sins in our life and responsibly embrace instruction from others, even when it might feel painful or intrusive.

"Love like you've never been hurt" is a lifelong, high, and challenging bar to strive after. Asserting that hurt is inevitable to our relationships seems difficult enough. Beyond this we are also challenged to protect against allowing the scars of hurt of one relationship to infect the potential fruit and joy of a different relationship. While "forgive and forget" is a characteristic of an all-loving and eternal Creator, as a frail human, I'm much less capable of the forgetting part. I am capable, however, of taking active steps to move forward. With due regard to the nature of an offense, professionals universally speak of how critical it is for people to launch a repair effort following any dust up. The proverbial olive branch may begin with an apology, but reaching out with vulnerability through the awkwardness, silence, or inevitable distance following a hurt is critical. One must arrest the damage and attempt to reverse any possible trends toward a negative or cynical mindset taking root. Continuing to reflect positively on shared history and keeping good memories at the forefront of our interactions helps to create more robust relationships that know of thriving times that will help create room for the grace we may need following a relational hardship.

As I hope to grow in my roles as a husband, father, and leader, it is important to go deeper in my understanding of what forgiveness, making changes, and moving forward looks like. Working to heal a relationship has observable hallmarks of action that are critical to healthy environments at both home and work. Organizational researchers have frequently published that effective work relationships supersede any administrative structure and note that informal networks are often relied upon, nearly exclusively, over administrative hierarchies to accomplish urgent team objectives. Authentic leaders—those who demonstrate some vulnerability and desire to serve something greater than themselves—understand the importance of making public and marked change following a breach of trust or visible offense. When a key leader has a moral failure or when a close friend breaches a shared value or trust, we look for a confessional spirit that wants to demonstrably pivot to a new direction. Moving past shame or embarrassment, whether corporately or individually, demonstrating a turning away from past behavior, and walking in a new direction provide the immediate steps of triage to stabilize a trauma and take the first steps toward recovery and healing.

I remember a football coach who became known for his fits of rage at his own coaches, players, fans, and referees. His lack of self-control was an embarrassment to the university and the fans. For a number of years, patterns of administrative discipline and coerced apologies continued. I recall many apologies he made to the fans and media. These public comments were mostly coerced and insincere repair efforts generally devoid of any penitence intended to alter his own behavior in a new direction. Essentially, he communicated, "I am sorry if you were upset or offended by anything I may have done." If I was his instructor pilot, his grade sheet would clearly point to a lack of emotional maturity: "Unsatisfactory: student not receptive to instruction." The coach failed to acknowledge his glaring patterns of misbehavior and shortcomings, and he never expressed a heartfelt desire and plan to change. Rather, his pride impeded any true remorse or personal responsibility, and he blamed the problems on the fans and administrators whom he condescendedly regarded as too fragile for his leadership style. The coach was eventually fired. He repeated the same dysfunctional and angry demeanor, leaving his next team in a disarray of recruiting violations and penalties, only to be fired after a single season by yet another school. Avoiding the true nature of his problem—a flawed character and an unrepentant heart—served as a public caution that changing geography fails to also change our hearts. As Thomas à Kempis shared in the 1400s, "wherever you come you carry yourself with you."[9]

Whether at work or home, effective relational repair efforts need to see a sincere pivot toward change with continued progress, however small, that gives hope for further improvement and strengthened relationships in the future. How a wounded relationship heals or advances is a complex problem that considers many questions, such as:

- How sincere is the other person at genuine personal transformation?
- Has this individual responded with authenticity and conviction?
- Is this person willing to turn and walk in a new direction, forsaking the previous behavior, or is he or she prideful or stubborn?
- Was the offense a fleeting moment of poor judgment or frailty or worse?
- Was the offense a revelation of a greater character flaw that requires some significant deconstruction and perhaps professionally assisted rebuilding?

On behalf of the victim, not every instance of forgiveness implies a full restoration to exactly what the relationship was previously. Some wounds, such as abuse, are examples in which forgiveness should not imply unqualified restoration. An additional question might be, when forgiveness is extended, is there a need for new boundaries or a new definition of the nature of the relationship?

Have you ever hit your thumb with a hammer? How did you react? Was there hollering, colorful adjectives, rage, or throwing of nearby objects? I remember working on a garage door opener, awkwardly leaning across a ladder, holding up the door with a circus broom directly above my beloved 1998 Honda Prelude—a great car, a modern classic. As my wife looked on, the garage door slipped from my hold and my balance failed. As I fell to the ground, I struck my surgically repaired knee on the concrete and the ladder bounced off the bumper of my car, leaving a scratch and dent. Hurt but feeling furious at this circus of events I caused, I stood up, kicked the ladder into the yard, and swung the broom like a bat across the brick corner of the house, breaking the broom and launching shrapnel into the yard. I looked over my shoulder just in time to see my wife slip through the door and close it behind her.

When encountering anger, whether ours or another's, a natural reaction is to "return fire," and often with an escalation in intensity. Like physical pain, emotional hurt or trauma can also present as anger. As leaders, we will inevitably be confronted with anger in a relationship. Wholeness, healing, new insights, patience, and often solutions will emerge if we approach the anger as an outgrowth of hurt or pain and not merely as an unprovoked attack.

To extend grace and forgiveness, to reach past our emotions and history to extend a repair effort, are nearly countercultural today. Even a minor offense or newly discovered injustice becomes grounds and permission to be angry and respond with words or actions that feel justified. President Lincoln had to extend his grace and forgiveness by taking unpopular steps toward unity countless times, much to the anger of more radical northerners. Countless speeches, legislative actions, and reintegration efforts sputtered along, contested for years after his death as part of a journey to the reunification of the Union. While noble to initially extend forgiveness to another, we may often find that the raw power of an offense will reappear in our minds, perhaps unwelcome and uninvited but assaulting our thoughts and feelings. And on each occasion, as grace becomes a habit, we relearn that forgiveness is an action, a verb, and a decision, not an emotion.

THUNDERBOLT TAKEAWAYS

- ⚡ True love is not fragile.
- ⚡ How are work or the demands of life affecting your relationships? Are you anticipating or recovering from a trauma to the relationship leg of your life stool?
- ⚡ Who in your life needs to hear "You are one of us; we know you, and for better or worse, you are connected to us, and you have a place"? Name them. How would you begin to draw them into a secure and healthy friendship that helps them feel seen and that they belong?
- ⚡ Broken relationships exist for nearly everyone. Which of your relationships needs your attention to be more healthy? Will you begin to move toward health with prayer for your heart and that of the other person? Consider sending a handwritten note or making a call or choosing another form of action as a first repair effort.
- ⚡ Relationships are our most worthy pursuit. Each morning, whether recalling Scripture or Satchel, that day we should strive to "Love like we've never been hurt."

5

DANCE

"Moderate strength is shown in violence,
supreme strength is shown in levity."
—G. K. Chesterton

"Dance like nobody is watching."
—Satchel Paige

I grew up in a house where laughing loud was authorized. Even today I am a loud laugher and loud talker, and our family relishes seeing whimsy. Whether a witty sign held up by a college student at a football game, my five-year-old son riding his bike down the street with a pasta strainer on his head so he could look like a robot, or watching sketch comedy, my family delights in humor and laughter.

When Satchel encourages us to "Dance like nobody is watching," he is communicating that joy and contentment fill a critical role in the balance and interconnectedness of our lives. I laugh as I look at a black-and-white picture of Satchel sitting in the locker room wearing only underwear and a hat, playing

43

the guitar and singing for his teammates. As an underwear guitarist and Hall of Fame pitcher, countless stories confirm Satchel had a zest for life and a sense of joy that was impervious to criticism and able to overcome trying circumstances. His advice to "Dance like nobody is watching" is challenging and instructive.

Successfully pursuing and finding contentment and refreshment must be unashamedly individual. Searching for joy and contentment based on what others have accomplished or what our culture may have deemed significant or satisfying should have no bearing on each of us determining what brings renewal or a refreshed perspective to our own souls. Notice I said that it *should* have no bearing. Unfortunately, it too often does. As with most tyrannical "shoulds" of life, we seem predisposed to mapping our life's success and fulfillment in a perpetual hallway of dissatisfied comparison with others. Social comparison theory points out that we almost exclusively compare ourselves with others who we identify as superior or higher in their success, beauty, or position on the social ladder rather than a parallel or downward social comparison. Social media saturates us and our children with infinitely "upward" and personally marginalizing comparisons. We need to cleanse our perceptions of the infection of upward comparisons and courageously push back against all unhealthy social norms, especially those that shout that our happiness depends on what others think or our social stratification depends on whether we possess the newest gadget marketed to provide us with "happiness."

Joy and contentment may not look like Satchel in his underwear and with his guitar—at least I hope not. However, finding your personal dance leg of the stool, perhaps after realizing the formulas others follow are unsatisfying, is critical for your stool to achieve a solid balance and have a utility that compliments and enriches the other two legs. Moreover, making room for the dance leg of our lives brings soul and vitality into our leadership roles, breathes joy into our hearts, and helps us model how to savor life's delights for those around us.

I don't recall ever seeing a two-legged stool. I doubt I could work or rest while trying to sit on such an unstable piece of furniture. In a performance-driven culture, the dance leg is the one most easily discarded, shortened, or ignored when other demands become too much. We've all been in the circles of those whose life and purpose only reside in a busy office or in perpetual servitude of their own children. Work and relationships are unquestionably important and, at times, may consume nearly the entirety of our time and attention. We've seen, and perhaps experienced, the heaviness of a life that lacks the fresh water of joy and the reinvigoration that pleasure and simple laughter bring in life's difficult seasons. And we may always wrestle with whether or not we're "doing enough." But we must redefine pleasure, rest, and healthy self-interest as more than juvenile time off but as investments in our long-term health and effectiveness and in our capacity to connect more deeply with others.

My son, Jake, enjoys sports. For his fifth birthday, he told us he wanted a football birthday party. My wife called a friend whose husband was the head baseball coach at the local NCAA D-II university to get some special access to their facilities and to plan an appearance by the celebrity mascot, Mo the Mule. Mo is a red mule in a sports jersey the kids love. If you happen to visit the area, however, I warn you not to call Mo a donkey. With the locals, that designation can turn violent surprisingly quickly.

The special day finally arrived, and we gathered up a neighborhood of boys and girls and all of the helmets and jerseys we could find for a hard-hitting birthday party. Heading to the family van stuffed full of friends, Jake looked up and asked me, "Dad, where is your uniform?"

Cross-checking my own gym shorts, T-shirt, and running shoes, I told Jake I was dressed and ready to go.

"No, dad," Jake said. "Where is your uniform? The one in the closet."

I was puzzled for a moment and then realized that he had seen a pair of football pants and a jersey that a college roommate had given me as a gag gift. The little town of Butte, Nebraska, where Jake's grandmother was raised, was consolidating high schools and had auctioned off their old uniforms. Thinking that I would want some Butte sports memorabilia, my buddy bought me a 1980s style uniform for my "collection." As a consequence, extremely small and shiny maroon football pants and a matching old mesh jersey were buried in my closet corner. Hesitating, I looked at Jake's expectant face and thought, *No problem, if that's what Jake wants, that's what I'll wear*. Several uncomfortable minutes of contorting limbs, working into a musky sweat, and testing tensile strength limits of the stitching soon followed as I worked to pack my legs and large backside into the shimmering pants. After adding the jersey to my attire, my wife's cackles confirmed my uniform to be comically revealing and yet short of anatomical or public indecency.

Now crammed into my uniform, we headed for the football field with our preschool-aged players buckled into a convoy of minivans. As we parked, I grabbed Jake's hand, and we happily headed across campus to the athletic fields. Walking together, several college students passed and smirked at my uniform. Then there were the looks and semi-concealed laughter of several baseball players, cheerleaders, and even some of the coaching staff. I don't embarrass easily (although my wife would prefer I did), but even I began feeling a bit sheepish.

Perhaps sensing my awkward discomfort, Jake looked at me and said, "Dad, are you embarrassed?"

Everything stopped for me. This was a dad moment. My son had asked me a question that I knew I had to get right. This was one of those teachable times that help shape the character and worldview of your child. I could hear theatrical stringed music cueing in my mind as I readied myself for a triumphant parenting moment of speaking wisdom into the life of my child. I leaned over Jake and began to convey the wisdom of Satchel Paige, expounding on the ideas of the dance pillar of our lives and how contentment should be determined only by us. This was his special day, I exhorted, and no one else's opinion was going to determine our happiness and joy. We would give no one that power over us! Thinking I had come through by reassuring my son of my love and our happiness, he just looked at me puzzled.

With a shrug he said, "No, dad. I mean, you've got a hole in your crotch."

In spite of the hole, I hope embracing whimsy and nurturing the dance leg of our stool found some place in Jake's heart.

Some of the world's best have modeled an interconnected life that made room for joy, refreshment, and rest. These leaders made routine investments in themselves as a means of continuing ahead in their roles. President Abraham Lincoln, for example, was known to cherish laughter and storytelling and enjoyed regular walks and conversations among soldiers. Former Secretary of State Dr. Condoleeza Rice, gifted in so many ways, described in *Golf Digest* her growing love of golf while working under the intense klieg lights of Washington, DC.[10] Sir Winston Churchill was known to paint landscape scenes and swim. American President Ronald Reagan began his days in the White House reading the funny pages. Nobel prize-winning Army Chief of Staff General George Marshall (and future secretary of state) maintained a sacred regimen of early morning horseback rides during his six years of leadership through World War II. These renowned world leaders recognized and protected their needs for laughter and reflection, refreshment, and a sense of contentment in their lives. How much more necessary is it for the more common of us to need and seize opportunities for revitalization? Perhaps the wisdom and model of self-care of these exceptional leaders will inform our own.

More than simply following a good example or embracing the interconnected view of our work, relationships, and health, we must realize and act on the fact that rest is critical to human health. A day of rest, a sabbath, is important enough to warrant a biblical command: "Remember the Sabbath day, to keep it holy" (Exodus 20:8 NASB). Rest builds the opportunity for reflection and reordering our priorities. Rest is a critical tool for securing a contentment that remains unhurried.

Joy and purpose are most exemplified by those able to find a contentment that outsizes any life circumstance. The apostle Paul tells us:

> I am not saying this because I am in need, for I have learned to be content whatever the circumstances. I know what it is to be in need, and I know what it is to have plenty. I have learned the secret of being content in any and every situation, whether well fed or hungry, whether living in plenty or in want. I can do all this through him who gives me strength. (Philippians 4:11–12 NIV)

Paul understands that personal strength and resolve have inherent limits. But by making room in our spiritual lives for a growing journey of faith that connects us with Christ, the seemingly impossible becomes possible with the Lord's blessing, wisdom, and orchestration. And this journey requires regular periods of rest and reflection. As God tells us in Psalms, "Be still, and know that I am God" (Psalm 46:10 NIV).

My college professor shared this simple story to help us students who were busy writing theses papers, working too many jobs, and sleeping poorly for months. In the time of the American pioneers, a young frontier man proposed to a young lady. (I imagine a scene from the TV show *Little House on the Prairie* for those old enough to remember.) The young lady accepted, and the young man excitedly purchased a new axe to log trees and build the cabin they would eventually share together. Awaking the first day, the young man was able to cut down ten trees. Keeping the same schedule, on day two he was only able to cut down nine trees. Day three saw his efforts reduced to eight trees. The negative trend continued over the following weeks to the point where the frontier fiancé began work at dawn, blistered and bloodied, swinging to the point of exhaustion and reduced in spirit, energy, and effectiveness. His production dropped all the way to cutting down only one tree a day. Perplexed and humbled, he confided in his future father-in-law, asking him what he might be doing wrong. The wise man replied, "Son, you need to sharpen your axe." The young man needed to take regular time-outs to at least sharpen his axe.

As it failed to occur to the frontier man, our western instinct often fails to view the nurturing of joy, contentment, and rest as a worthy investment. For a driven culture, healthy self-interest becomes confused with selfishness, and guilt becomes an unwelcome sidekick when we overestimate our value or responsibilities. As a leader, husband, and parent, if I can't care for myself, how can I empathically take care of those entrusted to me? Further, if I am unable to model a healthy life balance that connects well-being and rest, it is unlikely my loved ones will make room in their lives to dance, let alone have a sense that joy and whimsy should have a place in their lives.

Unfortunately, our rise-and-grind work culture worships productivity to the point that activities purely for pleasure, such as a trail walk, a leisurely round of golf, or reading a spy novel, have to become competitive or become part of a quest for endless self-improvement. In other words, activities to enjoy must be turned into something more, something greater—otherwise, they just aren't worth our time. Now, I love to compete, cross things off my list, try new challenges, and get better at something, but pursuing pleasurable activity for pleasure's sake alone must be worthy of our time too. The difficulty I have with making a routine habit of refreshment is reflected in the amount of time it takes for me to disengage from the emails, text messages, and ruminations of work and become fully present on what's meant for play and rest. The connectedness of our culture, combined with both our actual and perceived ability to have an impact, make any sabbath rest or disconnection increasingly difficult. Today's employers send a mixed message by encouraging employees to take their vacation and prioritize their family while also issuing a company provided cell phone to both broaden and ease employee accessibility. As work from home initiatives move from the hippy tech sector to common employer practices, the challenge for employees is to find a protected harbor from within their own homes and on their calendar where rest and recreation are not intruded upon by perpetual availability.

THUNDERBOLT TAKEAWAYS

We know that a two-legged stool has no real utility and that the third leg, dance, brings energy as it also sharpens the work and relationship areas of our lives. Let's take a life inventory, perhaps inviting those we love to help us, and determine if the dance leg has any place in our lives: Do we actually believe that rest and recreation are healthy? If so—and I certainly hope so—then what kinds of activities might help jump-start a dormant or neglected need for rest and refreshment? Here are some questions that can launch your assessment:

- ✗ What delights you like a five-year-old at your own flag football birthday party?
- ✗ Do you allow whimsy into your life, workplace, and home? If so, list some examples.
- ✗ What do you do for fun? Does this activity refresh you or exhaust you?

What activities, hobbies, or interests can you speak about for hours with comparative expertise and have more energy at the end of the conversation than you did at the beginning? When I've asked other people these questions, I've seen eyes sparkle and voices pitch in excitement as they mention activities such as rock climbing, stamp collecting, reading, dog training, and volunteering. Do you have anything like this in your life or something like it you can add?

As you consider what I'm suggesting, let me propose a few cautions.

✗ Does your preferred activity require an inordinate amount of time or finances that generate financial or time stressors in your home?

I often think of a college friend who, newly married, chose to continue playing on three separate softball teams, which required a good deal of travel and tournament teams nearly year-round. His absence as a husband and selfish use of time reflected an ongoing imbalance that contributed to the unfortunate end of his young marriage.

✗ Are you a better and refreshed wife, husband, friend, leader, or employee after spending time in your chosen method of dance?

I think of golf when I consider this question. I love to golf. More specifically, I love to play good golf. And that doesn't happen real often. Golf can begin to take too long, be too hard, or cost too much. But I enjoy the beauty of the courses, being outside, and the challenge of the sport. Like most golfers, I'm always seeking an advantage to gain accuracy or distance. That said, I also recently realized that I gained a lot of distance with my new irons: they go even further when I throw them in disgust. Sometimes I end up rushing around the course to hurry up and get home while sculling pitch shots over the green and perpetually losing to a game of me versus the scorecard. I confess that I don't always return home or go back to work the next day refreshed. I can play rounds of golf that don't make me a better person, whether as a husband, dad, commander, or Christian. So I adjust my expectations, alter the game, and apportion time differently for golf to be refreshing. If and when that fails, I need to choose something else to do.

⋏ Are you better, sharper, and refreshed following your time of dance, or are you poorer, red-faced, and absent?

Quite regularly, I hear how people want to "get back into it" or plan to reenter what they love "after things slow down" or postpone that fun "until retirement." There are definitely seasons of life when a healthy regimen of sharpening your axe might be abbreviated. Nevertheless, protecting time for refreshment and moving toward that becoming an indispensable routine are critical to finding and savoring joy in life. Finding what gives you joy brightens your outlook and points you in a direction to find that occasional cool drink of water. Unlike the frontier man, we should understand that routinely apportioning time and money to nurture the third leg of our stool is a critical investment that will sharpen and bring to life the other two legs of our stool and provide the lifeblood of interconnection that brings purpose and balance to life.

When Jake asked if I was embarrassed, his question taught me that over-concern with what others think is a learned trait. Neither he nor any of his pre-school friends had any concern about what they looked like or what the passing students thought. My self-regard was just that—mine. While I want my children to be empathetic, an excessive preoccupation with what others think is a flawed and dizzying internal dialogue. I wonder if this preoccupation with self and others starts from a middle school obsession of fitting in, finding a group, getting labeled, or owning the right brands of stuff. Some of us never grow out of this stage and spend a lifetime chasing joy and contentment based on income, rank, job titles, enviable vacations, kids' accomplishments, or possessions.

Always one to push against culture, Satchel encourages us to mature backwards to the carefree spirits of five-year-olds at a birthday party who solely define and hold the power to what brings them joy. And then they march toward the football field like nobody is watching.

Jake's fifth birthday.

Whimsy in our living room.

6

EXPECTATIONS:
THE GOOD, THE BAD, AND THE UGLY

"We cannot solve our problems with the same thinking
we used when we created them."
—Albert Einstein

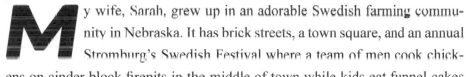y wife, Sarah, grew up in an adorable Swedish farming commu-
nity in Nebraska. It has brick streets, a town square, and an annual
Stromburg's Swedish Festival where a team of men cook chick-
ens on cinder block firepits in the middle of town while kids eat funnel cakes
and ride the dizzy teacups. Her busy weeks growing up revolved around being
a essential member in every school sport, activity, band, and club. Fellow class-
mates especially needed individuals to have enough participants to field a team.

In most homes, and in Sarah's childhood home after busy weeks of activities, Saturday mornings are a chance to recover and sleep late, read a few
newspapers, and sip coffee together. But Saturday mornings in my childhood
home were to be attacked and conquered. Our family was often up early
stalking garage sales for the "good stuff," enjoying a big country breakfast at

Hardees, and racing through yard chores so we could attend and participate in various YMCA games.

Sarah and I never talked about what Saturday mornings would look like after we were married. The subject never came up during premarital counseling sessions. We had different histories, and with no conscious effort, expectations had sprouted that neither of us had given voice to. Glowing in the early months of marriage (which is how I remember it), I recall blissful happiness mixed with a period of routine Saturday mid-day tension. Sarah would savor the morning, as she was accustomed, and I assumed a happy marriage meant every waking moment was spent together and that Saturdays were a chance to get ahead. I would bite through my nails as some of my world-saving to-do list would be postponed or not addressed at all. And a cool mutual frustration would find a way into our weekend of marital harmony. Expectations are like that, growing naturally like flowers and weeds, some to be nurtured and pruned while others need to be ruthlessly removed to enable fruitful health.

As the LPA (Lieutenant Protection Association) Commander with the 75th Fighter Squadron, one of my critical jobs as the snack-O was to keep the kegerator clean. Mold would grow in that funky little fridge with no effort, no purpose, and no attention from me. It was part of my job to clean it out. Like the unwanted and gross goop in the kegerator, personal expectations can formulate and rapidly grow completely absent of our attention or effort. Unattended, irrational, or unrealistic expectations can quickly grow unruly and begin to choke out our own contentment, confuse our sense of purpose, and diminish our quality of life. We cannot control many of life's circumstances, so sometimes we cannot meet the expectations that we or others put on us. Still, properly groomed expectations are a powerful tool to shape our mindset and ability to overcome hardship, adapt to changes, energize our pursuit of dreams, and remain optimistic in a world inundated with negative news.

Denmark is a small European nation that has dominated the Eurobarometer and world map studies as the happiest nation on earth. Equivalent in latitude to the Hudson Bay, I imagine Denmark has short days with gray skies requiring lots of wool sweaters. Unbelievably, nearly two-thirds of Danes self-report being "very satisfied" with their lives, while the nations surrounding Denmark score themselves much lower, even though they show no significant statistical differences in income, marriage rate, high tax rates, or weather to that of the Danes. Reported in the *New York Times*, *The Atlantic*, and several research journals, Denmark's near thirty-year domination of the polls was a puzzlement to researchers. Coupled to the happiness research and dating as far back as 1980, other survey data was collected on the expectations of participating nations. Remarkably, the most credible explanation for the secret key to Dane happiness turned out to be "Low Expectations." That's right, Danes carried the lowest expectations of happiness for the upcoming year but scored as the number one nation in the life satisfaction survey. Equally stunning and serving as an inverse confirmation of the findings, Turkey and Italy self-reported the highest expectations for the upcoming year yet scored the lowest on the happiness survey. Only 12 to 15 percent of their populations reported that they were very satisfied with their lives. Ongoing research has further redefined and segmented happiness barometers, and still Denmark persistently remains among the top happiest places on earth.[11]

It seems rather un-American or even soft to consider reducing our expectations. I can't imagine the tourism offices sending postcards that proclaim "Come to America . . . and be disappointed." Yet there is a profound correlation between our beliefs and expectations, the events we encounter and the consequences that follow. Expectations are those habits of thought and mental models born from life experiences, education, and upbringing that exist in all of us. Expectations, missed or met, are more easily seen in the physical realm. Missing a step at the bottom of the stairs or losing your footing on an icy path provide immediate pictures of when an expectation is not met. Mental expectations are occasionally as obvious in their fulfillment or failure, but at a more nuanced level, they really provide the lens through which we interpret life's events and the engine by which we move toward contentment and purpose or retreat to victimhood and feelings of injustice.

The Danes have learned somehow to prune expectations in a manner that hastens their mental health, happiness, and satisfaction. Hoping to live a life capable of purpose, happiness, and contentment amid seasons of triumph or defeat and every season in between begs us to open our individual kegerators and see what's growing inside. Unattended expectations, being neither pruned nor cultivated, can result in a vast wasteland of disappointment, anger, and entitlement.

On the other hand, irrational expectations can have an equally profound negative impact on our health. As Henry Ford famously said, "Whether you think you can, or you think you can't—you're right."

Our expectations have many layered characteristics, both positive and negative. To help us sort them out and to enable our pruning, pulling, and nurturing, I group expectations like three triplet girls I knew as a child: the Good, the Bad, and the Ugly. In the chapters ahead, we'll identify the positive or negative characteristics of each type of expectation and how our lives can be shaped by them.

THUNDERBOLT TAKEAWAYS

In the meantime, let's focus on the expectations placed on you in your home when you were growing up.

- How often were you expected to work at chores?
- What were you expected to do with your money?
- What kind of grades were expected of your schoolwork?
- Were you expected to attend church or another place of worship? If so, how often?
- Were there expected roles or responsibilities for different members of the family? What were yours, and how did they compare with those of other family members?
- Did any expectations just "exist" without actually being spoken?
- Did you get to anticipate fun or vacations or rewards in your formative years?
- How have you either continued with the same expectations or changed them from your upbringing?

7

THE GOOD:
GOLF AND THE JAVELIN

*"I learned that it is better, a thousand-fold, for a proud man to fall
and be humbled, than to hold up his head in his pride and fancied
innocence. I learned that he that will be a hero, will barely be a man."*
—George MacDonald, *Phantastes*

I grew up playing golf with my dad. He had a set of clubs cut down for me when I was a young child, and we still enjoy playing to this day. I never really committed to regularly practicing what I learned from a professional golf instructor, lessons designed to turn me into a good player. I've generally settled into less than a once-a-month golfer with some ocassional opportunities to play a few days in a row.

As a college student, I remember being home for summer break and golfing with a mentor from church. At the course, we were paired with a twosome of players we had never met. Strangely, I got off to a hot start and was two under par after only three holes. I thought, *Today is the day! I could shoot even par! Seventy-two or better, here I come!* I was laughing and having fun, my friend was rooting for me, and the twosome we just met were impressed.

But then, I promptly double bogeyed hole four out of the sand trap to move back to even par. Mad at botching my golden start, I swung out of my shoes on hole five and bombed a drive over a fairway sand trap. I flipped a lob wedge to 3 feet, and my confidence and expectations soared again to professional heights as I thought, *Three birdies in the first five holes? Who does that?*

Then my short birdie putt lipped out as a miss. I stepped into a full end over end golf club throw of my putter. I've tossed clubs before—a little under-handed flip toward a bag or something else. I used to think it was funny. This, however, was not that kind of toss. This was a full throw accentuated with a grunt. The sun glinted softly off the shaft as the putter began a slow parabolic descent before crashing into the golf cart, the club fragmenting into several pieces. Somehow an afternoon of golf now became a javelin throwing field event. The twosome of strangers stood frozen, wondering what this crazy kid might do next and if they should fear for their own safety.

As we walked up to the next tee box, I laughed at myself and tried to loosen the tension. One of the players with us asked me what I was studying in college. With a smirk of embarrassment and irony I replied, "Biblical stud-ies." We laughed as I explained I was merely an undergraduate so perhaps I hadn't yet learned what I needed. I also explained that the spring semester of the anger management coursework was full. Coincidentally, I think that was the same day I had a growing suspicion that flying fighter jets might be a better vocational fit than pastoral ministry.

Good expectations need to be *realistic*, not necessarily constrained to an easy or given outcome that doesn't make room for hope or improvement. Expec-tations should deal in the realm of the possible. Different from individually designed goals, expectations innately have an autonomous drive feature within us, and we universally overlay these expectations onto businesses, governments, sports teams, weather reports, or other nations over which we have zero control.

My golf score expectations were not part of a process of systematic goals and improvement. Rather, my expectations that day rocketed right past realistic and challenging to delusional in a span of three holes. A round of seventy-seven would have been a realistic challenge for my skill set and would not have accelerated my complete meltdown for the rest of the day by hole five. Realistic expectations are not to be interpreted as dream killers. Unlike those countries who continually fall short of their expectations and become unhappy, accurately seeing our expectations realized or exceeded can build a momentum of successes that refine our ability to clearly see how our expectations influence our well-being as well as give us a clear path of what future happiness can look like.

Well pruned expectations must also be *optimistic*. Resilience has become a critical thread among military leaders since the terrorist attacks on 9/11 as decades of perpetual and wearying combat deployments have had a very human toll on service members and families. Resilience is also a common theme throughout the human services community as they attempt to reinforce those qualities that enable one's ability to recover from and operate through difficult, unforeseen, or even unjust circumstances with healthy coping mechanisms. If there is such a phase as *optimistic realism*, resilience hinges on a hope and faith that knows, at its core, that a better life is possible while remaining clear-eyed about the challenges and realities that exist. Clear-eyed optimism is not a delusional detachment that avoids the difficult realities of life seeing only clouds made of cotton candy and rivers that flow with chocolate. Rather, an inspiring realist can acknowledge that hardships and injustices exist and that they may strike each of us at different times to our core. But optimism becomes a choice to engage the hardship and make strides toward recovery and improvement. I have seen senior leaders take the stage in both my military and commercial experiences and avoid bad news as they miss opportunities to be empathetic and publicly acknowledge a mess. Their actions completely undercut their own credibility. The teams they lead come to see them as out of touch as they struggle and often fail to inspire people to give of their best. Evading bad news also forfeits the opportunity to set a path that might correct a situation, demonstrate a commitment to courageous engagement over avoidance, and lay the footings to inspire genuine wins and progress—all of which build more momentum.

On a personal level, being optimistic doesn't mean that we never struggle with pessimism or question a purpose, outcome, or strategy. Some of our greatest leaders, amid the most desperate of circumstances, struggled to deny defeatism and rally hope in their own hearts and those of their followers. Former British Prime Minister Winston Churchill divulged in early letters to his wife that he felt nagged with the "black dog" of despair. Many historians believe that he routinely battled mild depression throughout his career.[12] Yet his bottomless reservoir of optimism and resiliency led and inspired an indominatable fighting spirit for England in World War II. General George Washington had private concerns that his army of Continentals might lose the revolutionary war. He went so far as to direct his estate manager to prepare his personal papers to move to safety in case he was defeated by the British and they were to send forces to destroy his home. A great little article by Major M. L. Cavanaugh of the Modern War Institute at West Point discusses the mental outlook of several historical supreme commanders during the direst of circumstances.[13] As the leaders have modeled, optimistic realism must be first won and cultivated in our own minds before being able to inspire and lead others, especially leading those little ones who may be eating chicken fingers at your kitchen table.

A final quality for healthy expectations is that they should be growth oriented. Most college football coaches speak frequently of their players' need to commit to their program and buy in to giving consistent and high levels of effort over a long journey of continuous improvement. While a win-loss record can be a cold, harsh, and immediate picture of success or failure every Saturday afternoon, as you watch coaches rebuild a program you begin to see their other metrics of success—incremental measurements taken as part of a process of building excellence that will hopefully be reflected in a more positive win-loss record. Weight-room scores and performance indices are tracked, as are sprint times, body fat percentage, team GPA, recruiting effectiveness, game-film grades, graduation rates, and countless other variables. When stacked together, these measurable variables and their goals comprise "the program." Growth oriented goals allow for layers of progression and multiple opportunities to embrace a process of encouraging little wins that help carry players to the mountaintop to which they are striving.

I remember my wife supporting her friend who wanted to run a local half marathon. My wife had been a good track athlete and was willing to run and train very early in the morning to help her friend toward her mountaintop goal. As they improved and got stronger, each training run extending their distances and accomplishing new goals, their habits of continuous improvement were rewarded with each outing. As they neared their race, Sarah's friend suffered a knee injury and couldn't run the half marathon. Of course disappointed, my wife had felt the health benefits of each training run, valuing each little win along the way. Unable to run the desired race did not negate all the positives leading to the end goal. Sarah won a road race in her hometown in the same season, and she and her friend ran a different half marathon a few months later. Had Sarah and her friend's view of success been so rigidly narrow to consider anything short of the desired race a failure, they would have discounted months of progress, all the little wins, and the joy of sharing a journey together based on a black-and-white unforgiving calendar. But does missing the desired competition invalidate the value of growth, perseverance, and improvement made through the training? In many regards, viewing expectations of ourselves, processes, family members, or a workplace team through the eyes of growth provides a healthier ramp of progression upon which small wins can move us toward a more holistic view of health versus a definitive score of perfectionism in which a sole event can determine victory or defeat.

Looking at the garden of expectations in my own life, I often come across weeds too late. After my frustration has bubbled up with someone failing to perform at what I consider an obvious standard, I can then see how I was wrong in my initial expectation. When my idealized mental picture isn't realized, my anger will quickly cast off any and all benefits accrued on the journey toward the long-term goal. Or looking at my own shortcomings or slow rates of improvement, I struggle to comprehend that goals, improvement and even discipleship are better characterized as a long walk in the same direction than an abrupt sprint of exertion with an immediate desired result.

Busy gardeners are out there every day weeding, cultivating, pruning, or stirring up the soil. There is work to be done, and they are getting it handled whether they see initial benefits or not. In the center of the city in which I live, there are flower fields. When we moved here in August, we saw only orange dirt ringing a hillside in town. We saw trucks and workers move up and down the hill. They were moving dirt, putting plastic in different places, and moving watering hoses. For eight months I only saw orange dirt. But when spring arrived, people visited by the carload to walk tulip fields planted that ring a hillside with brilliant banners of colors and a US flag of flowers a few football fields in size. Various other patterns of vibrant color struck onlookers with their beauty. If those gardeners walked away for months at a time, there would be profound consequences to their inattention. Likewise, ignoring how our beliefs and experiences drive what we expect of ourselves and others creates choking weeds that require some effort to remove. Perhaps our fields have been overrun by them.

THUNDERBOLT TAKEAWAYS

Grab your pruning shears and gardening gloves and let's attend to the garden of the expectations that can drive our own happiness and contentment in work, relationships, and spiritual growth. Are you like the Danes with happiness present in your life as an outgrowth of an encultured healthy attention to expectations? Or are you struggling like our Italian and Turkish neighbors who seem to simmer with a frustration that life never lives up to what it should?

- ✈ What expectations do you have of yourself, your home, relationships, or work?
- ✈ Are they reasonable and realistic? How can you tell?

Ask yourself, are you inexplicably angered anew by an extended family member who has never showed a depth of interest in you when he or she retreats once again to a corner of the house or never asks what is going on in your life?

Are you triggered when your boss at work for the upteenth week fails to say thank you for your diligent efforts?

Do you get upset or frustrated with yourself when you miss another personal goal?

If any of these questions marshal a positive response or link you to other situations that bear some resemblance to these, perhaps your expectations are unreasonable and unrealistic. You may, for instance, irrationally believe that you can somehow control the behaviors and interactions of others. Or, like my golf club throw, your hopes for personal improvement may have rocketed past realistic "stretch goals" and the investment that getting better entails.

✗ Are your expectations oriented to continued development, a process of improvement, or personal growth?

There was a popular custom motorcycle builder and master marketer by the name of Jesse James of West Coast Choppers. As of this writing, he has added six thousand dollar custom kitchen knives to his repertoire. Anyway, as he built more popular and more radical motorcycles and his TV show soared in popularity, I remember an episode of *Monster Garage* in which he said, "I like to try and build something that is a little beyond what I think I can do."

Jesse the motorcycle builder, and now my helpful life coach, provides a perfect frame for realistic, optimistic, and growth oriented expectations. We can challenge ourselves to improve a little beyond what we think we can do. We can commit ourselves to ongoing improvement that will help us achieve our best as we step above what we're accustomed to expecting of ourselves or others and the organizations to which we belong.

✗ What are some healthy expectations that have provided a greater contentment in your life or stretched you to pursue a better version of yourself?

Perhaps you are in the midst of a difficult season, harassed by the black dog of defeat or sensing that you are inadequate for your current role or struggling to stay afloat as the world billows trouble around you. A greater reward, richer fulfillment, or even smoother procedures for a team are near enough our grasp that enduring seasons of trial become bearable when our eyes and heart are fixed and hopeful for what is to come.

I've recently been pruned—encouraged to have higher expectations of myself and to learn a healthier way for filling a role in which the Lord has entrusted me. Realizing that pruning, although painful and seemingly destructive, results in greater fruit in our lives provides a purpose to the discomfort. Too often we prefer to avoid the introspection or the scary trust in another to be confronted with what needs to be pruned from our lives. I am encouraged that the process modern-day leaders talk about as critical feedback, stretch goals, and continuous improvement were authored long before by a Gardener who truly desires for us to bear prodigious fruit as we were designed. Healthy living requires pruning, even in those areas of our lives that are already fruitful. As Jesus said, "I am the true vine, and my Father is the gardener. He cuts off every branch in me that bears no fruit, while every branch that does bear fruit he prunes so that it will be even more fruitful" (John 15:1–2 NIV). May we yield to the Gardner supreme and thereby experience growth and fruit that we could never achieve solely on our own.

8

THE BAD:
UNDERWEAR AS EARMUFFS

"Bad decisions make for great stories!"
—Dozer, A-10 fighter pilot

"**B**ad decisions make for great stories." That's the wise counsel my friend Dozer mentored me with as we recounted another shared misadventure. Dozer was a great pilot, shade tree mechanic, and sage source of Georgian wisdom. Most pilot wives in the squadron would roll their eyes with any story that had Dozer's name involved. Most of the flyers, however, would smile in anticipation of what possible tale would be shared next.

Dozer had deployed with the army as a close air support expert for Operation Iraqi Freedom. His was one of the first vehicles to race onto the tarmac during the airfield seizure at Baghdad International Airport. A versatile warrior, he was also brave enough to wear a full pink bunny costume and ride a scooter with his date into the restaurant for the annual fighter squadron Christmas party. Some decisions are so bad that, like expectations, they must be completely cut out and removed because no redeemable quality exists. We shared a few of those decisions.

As we looked at how to cultivate good, healthy, and growth-producing expectations, we saw that the Master Gardener instructs us that fruitful, producing vines are cut back and pruned so they might be made evermore fruitful (John 15:1–2). Those things that are good in us can always be honed to be better, sharper, and more like Christ. Time-worn choices of past successes may need to be pruned to be reinvigorated for more fruit-bearing relevance today. Recall Jesus's words: "I am the true vine, and my Father is the gardener. He cuts off every branch in me that bears no fruit, while every branch that does bear fruit he prunes so that it will be even more fruitful" (NIV). Any vines that aren't producing life or aren't bearing fruit are cut out to wither, die, and be cast into the fire. As Jesus says, "If you do not remain in me, you are like a branch that is thrown away and withers; such branches are picked up, thrown into the fire and burned" (v. 6). That's pretty clear language. The Gardener wants results in the condition of our hearts and the fruit of our labor. Anything that gets in the way is to be removed. We're not to dress up dead or sinful areas of our lives with a fresh coat of paint or hide them behind the colorful, fruit-bearing areas of our lives. Rather than dilute energy from the whole vine and be distracted by a single dead branch, we are to ruthlessly remove things like selfishness, insecurity, greed, fear, pride, and lust from our lives.

The Master Gardener has planted us to bear fruit, to be productive, and to fulfill his calling and purpose in this life. The desired fruits of a Christlike spirit—love, joy, peace, patience, kindness, goodness, faithfulness, gentleness, and self-control (Galatians 5:22–23)—testify that our value and character are far richer than what we produce. The quality and diligence in which we invest our time and lives are to be done with an eternal purpose that glorifies him and impacts others. Having a spirit that loves others and is empathetic to meeting earthly needs surely must understand that being productive, even performing well at a job that no one else cares to do, is a great testament to character while also being productive in this world in preparation for the world to come. Some decisions or expectations choke out our productive fruit and have no redeeming quality. These must be discarded from our hearts and actions.

And so my buddy Dozer and I had followed the air force in different directions following Operation Iraqi Freedom. We rejoined at Barksdale Air Force Base near Shreveport, Louisiana to requalify in the A-10 as we were both returning to the Combat Air Force as pilots with the 303rd Fighter Squadron at Whiteman Air Force Base in Missouri. Finishing up our flying and academic coursework, we had left Louisiana for a week to prepare our homes for a delivery of household goods before returning to Shreveport for our final out-processing. I wanted to race down to Shreveport and back to be as available as possible for our move in at Missouri. I had already left two military moves completely to my wife to handle, and the prospects of a third appeared to me to have potentially nuclear repercussions. Dozer owned a small two-seat experimental airplane that he had left in Louisiana. I proposed a master plan to split the rental car and gas, saving Dozer some money, and then I could hitch a ride back with him to Missouri, thereby saving me countless hours driving through the switchback trails of Arkansas and across Louisiana. That was the last positive thought associated with this weed of a decision that should have been cast out and burned.

The small town we were moving to would not allow a one-way car rental, so I hitched a ride 90 miles north, the wrong way, to rent a car for our trip. Three hours and 180 miles into our "efficient" trip to Shreveport, I pulled back into our hometown to pick up Dozer for our nine-hour ride south. Finally on the highway, six hours later than we had originally planned, I started on the fastest possible route. Immediately I frustrated Dozer's plans as I learned my choice of routing would now bypass his opportunity for a "comfort stop" to visit his girlfriend in Arkansas. The cold and black drizzle of a December night followed us the entire switchback heavy drive through the Ozark Mountains until we arrived at our billeting rooms at 2 a.m.

Quickly finishing our out-processing, low clouds had rolled in over Shreveport that morning. We waited all day for the weather to clear. Approaching dusk, we finally determined the weather was close enough to legal visual flying rules that we would most likely stay alive. So we squeezed into Dozer's plane and took off into the cold winter air. An hour later, we were cruising into a headwind in freezing temperatures over the black mountains of the Ozarks, navigating with a Garmin road-map device designed for cars. From that we noted that there was absolutely no place to put the plane down in case of an emergency. And while a creative innovator, routine maintenance was not Dozer's strongest skill set. He had not weather stripped the rear glass of his cockpit, which allowed the cold air to accelerate from our prop wash through the rear glass and onto our backs and straight into our frozen souls. I reached into my duffel bag and pulled out some long underwear I had worn on the drive down. I used it to fashion ski masks to wrap around our necks and heads as we leaned toward each other to try and conserve some body heat. Cruising over the dark Ozarks, we laughed nervously about how embarrassing it would be if two combat-decorated fighter pilots crashed together in this tiny plane into the mountainous woods. Worse than death and the accelerant to our now loud laughter was the thought of my family trying to piece together why my body was found frozen in the middle of the woods amid aircraft wreckage and lying next to another now failed fighter pilot and why we both had our underwear tied around our heads.

We eventually landed in Missouri. A gusty below zero winter storm greeted us as we climbed out of the airplane. Heading home, we grabbed a bite to eat, and I told Dozer how much his half of the rental car and gas totaled. He then told me how much I owed for my half of the airplane gas and my portion of a class gift he had given to the training squadron on our behalf. I ended up paying three times more than it would have cost if I had patiently driven down by myself. And our trip was definitely more dangerous and took twice as long because of the long series of bad decisions we had made.

A Deeper Dive into the Weeds

The weeds in our lives might start as small distractions and seem unobtrusive enough. But given enough time or inattention, the negative impact of bad expectations will choke out our own ability to be productive, content, and available to support others. The bad types of expectations can take many forms. The tricky part is that we often view having very high expectations as good for driving us to be better, achieve goals, and soar with inspiration. But this doesn't make bad expectations healthy. Instead they can erode our relationships, our sense of self-worth, and our life satisfaction. Here are a few weeds that I think the Danes are particularly adept at pulling from their own gardens.

The Unrealistic

We all carry unrealistic expectations; it seems to be a component of the human condition. Humorously, one psychologist said the biggest unrealistic expectation is that people shouldn't have unrealistic expectations. Unrealistic goals can paralyze us when we are inevitably confronted with disappointment. They can also move us to negatively view ourselves and our capabilities, and to become cynical of others if our relationships fail to meet the template of unrealistic expectations we overlay on our lives. Oftentimes, when we see these expectations written on paper or see others try to apply them in their own lives, the flaws are obvious to us. However, when unrealistic expectations are a routine voice in our inner dialogue, a weed that we may have a lifetime of acclimation, they become more difficult to identify, and we may be less ruthless in their removal.[14]

Here are some examples of unrealistic expectations that may find a place in your garden that need to be torn out and cast into the fire[15]:

- "Everyone must like me." The reality is that we can't make everyone like us—no matter how hard we try. Even Jesus had people in his life who disliked him, even hated him (Luke 4:28–29; 6:11; 11:53; 19:47). If he had haters, what makes us think that we could be exceptions?
- "The world should be fair." This also is unrealistic because we can't control all aspects of the world to ensure that it operates consistently in the most fair manner. Not everyone lives by the same values, and in a world marked by brokenness or sin, we will witness and experience unfair things.

- "My golden years were supposed to just be golden." Well, the truth is that there are many transitions and challenges throughout life, including during the senior years.

Tightly connected to these types of thoughts are other examples of the paralyzing rigidity of unrealistic expectations that have a high need for control—a level of control that we often do not actually have in a situation. These weeds also include what I remember as the "Tyranny of the Shoulds," while they also block out the likelihood of risk-taking to avoid potential failure.

- "It's not okay to be depressed or anxious." Well, everyone struggles at some level with uncertainty and questioning whether or not we have what it takes to be successful or to meet the next challenge. Dwelling on or being convinced of our inadequacies or inability to affect our circumstances can be emotionally exhausting and leave us feeling drained. Accepting that these seasons are universally experienced parts of our human and frail condition can relieve the pressure that comes with chronically thinking, *I must be doing something really wrong.*
- "It's not okay to have painful feelings and thoughts." Allowing room for painful feelings and thoughts on the palette of our emotions doesn't mean we have to like those colors. We can want painful things to end as soon as possible. Even King David in the Psalms prays with a raw need for his pain or suffering to end (e.g., Psalm 70; 86; 109). Experiencing pain doesn't automatically mean that I've done something wrong or that I'm weak when I want hard things to quickly pass. It would be unhealthy to believe we should never experience painful feelings or thoughts or that they are never able to be instructive and purposeful.
- "I need to know what's going to happen." A natural instinct to want to know what's next can quickly become paralyzing if we incorrectly think we can control every outcome and deduce that all outcomes are a direct reflection of us and our abilities. Here is where hoping for something must be allowed to power us to span across the chasm of

the unknown. Otherwise, we sit idling in our own worry, fretting about all conceivable negatives and moving nowhere.

- "My spouse should know how I'm feeling without my needing to express it." Although a married couple may be one in spirit, mind reading is an unreliable communication technique. My wife realizes, perhaps with an occasional sigh, that I need words spoken in simple Crayola. Spoken words, even better than emojis, provide the most complete and detailed picture of the nuanced and complex "what" and important "why."

- "My kids should always listen to me." We see gifted adults, coworkers, and subordinates who don't always listen. So expecting still developing kids to have a higher standard of behavior is an unrealistic expectation. Focusing as a parent on listening and being emotionally warm to your children, providing a routine of structure as well as inviting excursions and future dreams, are more realistic methods to seeing your kids listen more.[16]

- "If my partner loved me, then they'd know how I'm feeling." This is actually a common and erroneous assumption. While all of us want to feel heard, chosen, and understood, expecting any human, even a precious loved one, to flawlessly intuit our feelings and appropriately respond is perhaps the most unrealistic expectation of all. I'm still learning about my wife and her needs, and we pay attention to each other. Nevertheless, sometimes we have thought that we knew what the other person was thinking or feeling, and we were wrong. No human being is infallible in their knowledge.

The Kudzu vine was introduced in the early twentieth century as a measure for erosion control due to it's aggressive rate of growth. Very soon the merits for the vine became a negative, and Kudzu was demoted to weed status. It's incredible growth of a foot per day, up to 100 feet per year, began suffocating native plants, crops, and timberland while competing for precious soil and moisture.

We cannot afford for our precious mental and emotional energy to be overcome with unchecked, unrealistic Kudzu-type expectations. While we are accustomed to highly effective, highly efficient software, phones, spreadsheets, food deliveries, and personal orders from the likes of Amazon, we must exercise caution against an unhealthy expectation that our human interactions can be equally orderly, sterile, and without conflict. The naturally experienced rhythms of learning to respond, respect, grow, anticipate, and love one another need permission, time, and protecton from aggressive and invasive unrealistic expectations.

The Unrelenting

Unrelenting expectations seem to be intertwined with American values of competitive ambition, industrious solutions, and an indefatigable work ethic. A challenge of these ideals is to search out how to balance ambition with peace, rest, and an enriched quality of life. Many of us are haunted by the thought that much of life is never quite good enough, whether we're thinking about work, marriage, family, or possessions.

One element of unrelenting expectations is an undercurrent of perfectionism—the notion that a perfect or idealized state of performance or achievement or a romanticized vision of a relationship must be fully realized for contentment or happiness to follow. In reality, perfectionism is a car hitched to unrelenting expectations that, although capable of pushing many individuals to various levels of what they think is success, quickly dismisses their achievements as it demands a new and higher standard to chase. Attention to self-care or investments in our relationships are quickly redirected to a merciless pursuit of perfection: scoring higher, making more, running faster, or looking better.

Several years ago my brother and I were hiking up from a small fishing village in Brazil over some steep cliffs on a peninsula to another vista point with access to the ocean. Climbing a muddy trail, with both of my surgically worked-on knees complaining, it seemed that we would never emerge from under the triple canopy covering the forest. We could occasionally glimpse how far we had climbed, looking back down at the village. The deeper we got into the peninsula, however, the less frequently we could assess how far we had traveled. Eventually we broke out to an incredible vista, seeing down the other side of the peninsular cliffs to see an amazing view of cliffs, rocks, forest, and a myriad of blues and greens in the water far below. We sat at the vista for a long time, savoring the view, the fruits of our climb, and studying how villagers dried out coffee beans and made the most intricate of cages for small exotic birds. And then we ducked back onto the trail to head down to the water, temporarily losing sight of our next goal but generously refreshed for the next challenge.

It's common among many of us to work desperately hard at parenting, our jobs, our marriage, or our education and then at some point on the trail, fail to stop and savor how far we've come. We may pause for one night of a celebratory dinner or obligatory picture worthy of our social media persona, but we may sense that we've only accomplished what many others have before us so we convince ourselves that it's time to tackle the next thing. We then quickly jump back onto the trail of grinding toward whatever might be next, losing the sight and inspiration of our progress. The tendency of people to gravitate toward a particular set point of happiness, following both positive or negative experiences, is known as the Hedonic Treadmill. While either recovering from a tragedy or celebrating a triumph or even a new standard of living, in a relatively short period of time people tend to return to their individual dispositions of optimism and satisfaction or pessimism and discontent. Although the Hedonic Treadmill is a commonly held phenomena, more recent studies have shown that about 40 percent of our happiness is dependent on our actions, thoughts, and attitudes. That means we are not victims of our historical mental gardening. We can turn over fresh soil, cultivate new thought patterns, and have the opportunity to walk in a contentment that is unique and novel. We don't have to live with pervasive dissatisfaction and unhappiness, including when it comes from around us, not just within us.[17]

As a Christian, I understand that there is value in hope and an expectation that God can intervene in our lives. I also realize that we are called to "take captive every thought to make it obedient to Christ" (2 Corinthians 10:5) and to train our minds accordingly. The work is not easy. At the same time, we must grasp the fact that for introspection and true character change to be effective, we dare not rely solely on white-knuckled willpower or psychology, leaning only on our own understanding and strength. Our abilities are woefully inadequate to the task and far less transformative than when we invite the hands of the Master Gardener to help shape our lives. We are truly dependent on him. As Jesus said: "I am the vine; you are the branches. If you remain in me and I in you, you will bear much fruit; apart from me you can do nothing" (John 15:5 NIV).

THUNDERBOLT TAKEAWAYS

With a spade in hand and hunger to cultivate a life that has an opportunity to live out and model contentment and happiness, here are some horticultural tips for your well-being[18]:

- ✔ **Give yourself permission to be human.** Accept your emotions, even including those we don't prefer, like fear, sadness, and anxiety. Rejecting them leads to frustration. Acceptance and a measure of personal grace might also need to be extended to your physical attributes, cultural peculiarities, or unique family dynamics.

- ✔ **Use the double standard technique.** I often notice that I have much less flexibility or grace for myself and my inevitable mistakes or shortcomings than I do for others. Consider what you might say to a family member or coworker who has fallen short of an expectation. Perhaps something like, "We're all human. Those kinds of things happen. We can fix it." Extending that same realism and self-compassion to yourself can begin to rewire your thought life.

- ✔ **Laugh and be curious about your own thoughts.** Smoothing out your own defensiveness with a self-deprecating laugh or even student-like curiosity about why you have come to believe something can provide levity and encouragement for personal growth. Not all personal flaws are dark and deep. In fact, most are not. Lumping them all together into what you deem an evil stew is unhealthy.

✗ **Who's the boss?** Reflect on your expectations and determine which ones are serving you, your goals, and your well-being. You'll likely find that at least some of your expectations have you indentured to the irrational and unrelenting. Consider how you can disassemble your fears and unreasonable expectations with data and facts and thereby purge them of their power over you. Be *their* boss. Don't let them rule you. And remember, as their boss, you can fire them!

Dozer and I likely could have realized very early in our plan, perhaps by even checking a weather forecast, that our expectations were unreasonable. If we had done this, we would have avoided the frustrations of our misadventure.

As with other areas of our lives, we may need to engage in a critical debrief. Journaling or taking notes regarding our thoughts and actions that drive our behavior are valuable tools that can help us bring coherence and understanding to why we do what we do. The evidence of the power of positive psychology has been a surprise to me as I tend to be a results-oriented skeptic. But the truth of Scripture encourages us to be wise, discerning, and shrewd while cultivating a thought life that thrives, free of weeds. And when we partner with the Great Gardener of the Gospel of John, our lives can be blessed and bless others with the fruit that matters most. The apostle Paul tells us the part we can play toward producing the best fruit:

> Finally, beloved, whatever is true, whatever is honorable, whatever is just, whatever is pure, whatever is pleasing, whatever is commendable, if there is any excellence and if there is anything worthy of praise, think about these things. Keep on doing the things that you have learned and received and heard from me and seen in me, and the God of peace will be with you. (Philippians 4:8–9)

9

THE UGLY:
THUNDERSTRUCK

"Everyone has a plan until they get hit in the mouth."
—Mike Tyson

I n 2008, I had requalified on the A-10 as a combat mission-ready (CMR) pilot after some years instructing in the T-38. My fighter squadron was returning to Bagram, Afghanistan in a few weeks, and we held a sacred CMR roll call in which a buddy and I would receive the 303rd Fighter Squadron's customized coin as a unique and exclusive token of our readiness status. It was a smaller than normal crowd that day. At one point in the fraternal liturgy, each of us are presented the coin (which, for mysterious reasons too dark and complex for this writing, is never again referred to as a "coin" by fighter pilots) and expected to make a toast.[19] I had come across a quote attributed to twenty-first-century philosopher and former boxer Mike Tyson. I raised my 30MM shell casing to the gathering of warriors, customarily filled to overflowing with the worst whiskey ever made, Jeremiah Weed, and said, "Everyone has a plan until they get hit in the mouth. Here's to flying a jet that hits the enemy in the mouth."

Although the A-10 is poised to deliver lethal blows, it also has a rugged design able to withstand profound battle damage and return safely overhead to friendly territory. While we humans may be slightly less resilient, we've all encountered the ugly, unexpected crises of life that seem to hit us in the mouth and cast our world into turmoil. I type this amid what many experts consider the worst global pandemic in a century, COVID-19. Fortunate to be insulated with a healthy family and weather that allows us to be outside during a statewide shelter-in-place order, it has been stunning to see the fragility and vulnerability of our nation's collective confidence, health, and economy.

We all know that life's unexpected happens, maybe even taking some teeth as it occurs. T-shirts and bumper stickers declare this truth: "Sh** Happens." Universally, life is full of these punches. Maybe we're absorbing a light jab that can be slipped, like an incorrect cell phone bill, a canceled flight, or failing to put the trash out for a day. Or maybe we get hit with a strong right cross in the form of a scary medical diagnosis, a layoff, the evaporation of our retirement plan, or a tragic decision made by a family member. I have several friends and acquaintances who were too late to pull the ejection handles and didn't get out of an airplane in time to save their lives. These events are a staggering blow straight to the soul. A potential knockout to those left behind. Such life punches are the last sibling of the expectations triplet I call the Ugly. They are always unexpected, and they pack a wallop from which it's hard to recover.

Fighter aviation, not unlike the work of businessmen, educators, home-makers, or any other industry, can be infinitely planned, updated, diagrammed, strategically plotted, visioned, or contingency rehearsed to a point of paralysis. Military leaders often note that no battle plan ever survives first contact with the enemy, while also lamenting that our national defense habit is to practice and prepare for the last war, not the next one. In my earliest training experiences, we had never discussed Afghanistan prior to 9/11. In the twenty-plus years since, reactionary training plans lumber forward to keep up with emerging Chinese and Russian threats as I have now flown in partnership with Baltic ground partners while also looking to World War II island-hopping tactics that again may be relevant to the increasingly contested Pacific.

The military community is exceptional at the tactical level of handling organizational agility. Prevailing leadership and management research discuss how winning organizations can rapidly and fluidly implement changes by developing a culture that expects adaptation and continuous improvement to be a hallmark of getting the job done. It is impossible to plan specifically for every contingency. But we can prepare for the unexpected. And that requires using principles that enable rapid and methodical responses during crises that will best posture us for personal and professional success. Much like a quarterback at the line of scrimmage who can mentally access hundreds of previously rehearsed plays, we can quickly scan the situation and call an audible that will put us in a good position to pull off the play. And even within the audible, there are varied options and flexibilities on how the play might be executed to have the greatest impact. Our initial, emotionally charged reactions to getting hit in the mouth play a role in determining the breadth or intensity of a problem. More important is the ability for our follow-on actions and communications to be a measured response versus a frantic reaction.

I was a T-38 instructor pilot in Texas for a few years early in my career. The T-38 is a 1950s era supersonic jet trainer that we typically use for advanced flying training for pilots heading on a track to fly fighter or bomber aircraft. It is a great, simple, and fun little sports car of a jet. Shortly after my son Jake was born, an email was sent out across the squadron looking for some short notice volunteers to fly in a four-ship formation flyby over Washington, DC. This particular event would also have a fifth jet as a potential spare aircraft and a photo ship for a ceremony with European and NATO nation leaders. I enjoy visiting DC and reluctantly mentioned the opportunity to my wife, Sarah. I was reluctant because our three-month-old son was leading the nation in bad colic. The poor little guy was uncomfortable much of the time and was exhausting us. Sarah knew I enjoyed the city and bravely encouraged me to volunteer.

Like most men encouraged to go on a road trip, I was certain I could smell a trap. I had learned several painfully important lessons about things you do not say to an exhausted mom trapped in a small house ten hours a day with a newborn and a toddler and with no other family members close enough to help. These lessons, embarrassingly, are 100 percent true. While packing for the road trip, do not ask, "Have you seen my swimsuit?" Following dinner at a famous restaurant located in our nation's amazing capital with friends who have no children throwing peas, do not remark to your wife that "My steak was really overcooked." And finally, while recovering in a king-size hotel bed, removed from the exhaustion of nightly infant feedings, do not mention that "The rooms in downtown DC are so small, this king-size bed hardly fits in here." With years of education and training, I still say dumb things. Sometimes in rapid sequence.

As our five-ship of T-38s set out from Texas to Andrews Air Force Base in Maryland, I was piloting the photo ship while my friend, also a pilot, was designated as the photographer and was seated in the aft cockpit. Somewhere over North Carolina, as my friend was flying, we entered some clouds. I sat in the front seat in my G-Suit and parachute with my left knee resting against the sheet metal box that contained the throttle quadrant. Suddenly, a huge flash of light illuminated the canopy. The left side of the jet's nose had been struck by lightning. With my leg resting against the throttle quadrant, a surge of static discharge travelled through the jet and through my knee, involuntarily snapping my leg straight and shocking a "sensitive region" of my body where the metal leg straps of the parachute harness and a G-suit button were touching. This is the point of a crisis when heroes say, "My training took over." As a fighter pilot trained to deal with precisely these types of emergencies, I calmly and in a tone reflecting the assurance of my faith, said to my buddy, "HOLY SH**! WE JUST GOT HIT BY LIGHTNING!!"

After our initial and emotional *reaction*, which was an expletive-filled matter of seconds of frantic checking of the engine gauges, flight controls, and our own body parts, we began the methodical and trained *response* of dealing with the unexpected. As we followed our trained maxims of dealing with an emergency— AVIATE – NAVIGATE – COMMUNICATE—we ran the steps of our emergency action checklist. The emergency itself was not a big deal, even though it was incredibly shocking (pun intended). No fires broke out, both engines and all avionics remained functional, and, to keep things interesting, we added in an emergency divert as our destination promptly closed due to a change to Air Force One's schedule. Although shocked, we were unscathed, arriving with the only minor damage being a charred exit mark on the left aileron.

Getting struck by lightning demonstrates that it doesn't matter how much energy has been put into avoidance, hand wringing, or worrying about bad things happening. Circumstances beyond our control can immediately and profoundly impact our lives. The sole matter of relevance is, what do you do now? When confronted with a crisis, perhaps bad news or crushing disappointment, how do you initially react? Is there full-blown panic and a resulting amount of collateral damage to those near you? Initial reactions defy a script of measurement, but the issue to consider is, are you capable of moving from the *reaction* phase to a methodical and measured *response* phase and how long does that transition take?

Success certainly isn't measured by being able to avoid hardship. In fact, it seems that in the cases of many of our nation's political and cultural leaders, the opposite is true. It is fascinating to learn the stories of inspirational leaders who overcame the unexpected and ugly blows to their personhood. Some examples: teen pregnancy (Oprah Winfrey), a best-selling author refused over thirty times on his first novel (Stephen King), a US president lost eight elections over his career and failed at business twice (President Lincoln), and initially, a failed businessman (Bill Gates). Nearly all of us, I'm sure, have experienced various levels of personal or professional hardship and have been forced to grow and respond to the inevitable circumstances of adversity, rejection, or failure.

While knowing nothing of sailing, I can appreciate the value of the saying that "smooth waters don't make for skillful sailors." Although preferring the easy and expected path, no skills are required when resting in place on a smooth and glassy surface. And these principles don't merely apply to a professional skill set. In the home, while living, sharing, and leading others, life is easy when there is no conflict, everyone is happy, and persons are good to you. Jesus Christ himself points out that when not challenged in our relationships to extend mercy or love to those whom it may be difficult, there is no growth: "And if you do good only to those who do good to you, why should you get credit? Even sinners do that much!" (Luke 6:33 NLT).

Most military training programs, as well as countless desired civilian occupations, require one to successfully complete a course of study and performance that is, by design, a pressure cooker of sorts. Within the air force and pilot training and years of subsequent qualification upgrades, most students adapt and eventually respond well to the demanding schedule, unending tests, flying evaluations, occasional failures, and daily corrections. I imagine the professions of many others to be the same. Resilience and perseverance are prerequisites to enter many demanding and desirable professions. Preparing pilots for stressful situations, such as aircraft emergencies or potential combat hostilities, is a key component of the training—training that most of us would prefer to remain merely preparatory. Not merely additive to flying the plane, the culture of always shifting schedules and instructors, new requirements, abrupt emergency quizzes, and unplanned weather or location changes stir up billows of turmoil that require students to quickly learn to sail or choose to remain in a safe harbor. Difficult training environments create a turbulent sea that begins to accelerate students beyond the immediate and often fruitless instinctive reaction phase while honing their ability to quickly sail to the response phase—a phase that typically demands quick yet precise decisions and actions. Through such training, we learn that we each have a limited capacity for how much emotional energy we can expend on things beyond our control. And given the complexity of the problems we are forced to solve, we should strive to make exceptional use of the people and tools at our disposal.

No one wants to get hit in the mouth, especially if Mike Tyson throws those punches. But we need to understand that we can learn much from each of the ugly and unexpected blows or crises we encounter. And the more we learn, the more capable we become to handle the next one, and the better equipped we become to support others. Much like combat life expectancies, the hope is to be equipped enough to survive the initial battles and blows to gain the most valuable asset, the prized education, and requisite bag of tricks that are reserved only for the savvy and experienced warrior. Fortunate for us, our savvy predecessors have outlined how to respond to emergencies, be it in the living room or from a raised platform amid a pandemic, economic crisis, or loss of public trust.

As student pilots straining to even properly start an aircraft, the maxims AVIATE – NAVIGATE – COMMUNICATE provide great guidelines for handling the Ugly.

AVIATE: *Stay alive.* Fly the jet first.

To AVIATE means taking the necessary initial steps needed to keep yourself or others safe and to stabilize a dynamic and possibly rapidly deteriorating situation. This is the triage care stage where staying alive is the goal, not trying to be perfect in every step of execution. If you encounter a blown tire on the highway, your immediate reaction is to control the car that is no longer performing properly, quite possibly requiring all of your initial attention and skills to simply avoid hitting another car or killing yourself as the car careens toward a bridge abutment. After safely removing yourself from traffic, then you can begin to ask questions about why this happened and where the spare is.

In the immediacy of a crisis, keeping a jet airborne or surviving an initial onslaught of punches is more critical than being perfect at analysis of a problem's cause, if the aircraft plunges into the earth due to misprioritization. Out of the cockpit, dealing with crises as a senior leader, including a midair collision involving a young fighter pilot, allegations of harassment between members while deployed, the moral failure of a previous unit leader, and a devastating health diagnosis for a coworker, my AVIATE step involved making immediate efforts for safety and stability. I may take these steps directly, or I may quickly involve the work of other professionals. What we should not do is presume those steps have occurred, that someone else has taken care of them so all is fine.

Once the crisis has passed and the situation has become stable, we enter the sustained survival phase and coping with specific results or changes due to the crisis. Here we can begin to analyze the situation. Questions I ask are:

What is working? What is broken? And what capability, resources, or tools are available that can help limp us to a safe place to land where a full diagnosis is possible? Speed is of the essence. Decisive action based on even imperfect information, as corporate and government leaders have learned following natural disasters, COVID-19, or 9/11, is most important. An immediate and courageous emergency action solution that may address just 50 percent of the problem is much better than waiting for more information to come in. The delay could bring greater damage, even death, and establishing a maxim for you or a team that is biased toward action is a critical investment, even if the initial results are merely adequate. Perfect becomes the enemy of the good and an unbearable speed brake when the situation needs to feel and see speed in a coherent response.

NAVIGATE: Where are we going?

From the jet, if I have a critical emergency, after keeping the thing in the air I want to point toward a safe place to land and, at least, be headed in a good initial direction.

On one occasion, I was leading a six-ship of jets home from Afghanistan. As we took off out of the Azores Islands and continued across the Atlantic, I knew that if I encountered any problem in the next few hours, I was at least going to turn the jet in the direction I wanted to go, toward the closest piece of land, even if I didn't know where precisely I would eventually pull in to park.

Likewise, when we encounter a relational or organizational crisis or trauma, we'll inevitably try to more clearly understand what has happened and the possible reason for and cause of the hardship's occurrence. And the road to recovery now that a workplace or family element has changed is to ask, where do we now want to end up? What may be a short-term destination that steps us in the direction of a longer term desired outcome? Perhaps a crisis is precisely the catalyst needed to compel overdue change or show that previous goals are no longer possible or even relevant. A devastated marriage, for example, may not have the strength to envision a long-term restoration, but limping toward a first counseling session can be a rapid first step in the right direction. Analyzing what a new normal might look like, including how our role at work or home or a corporate position in the ecosystem might be changed, are all preparatory steps for determining where we are going.

COMMUNICATE: Who do I need to tell or hear from?

The need for immediate and clear communication has never been more critical than today when global interconnectedness can accelerate a rumor or false crisis multiple times faster than the truth. Bad news never gets better with time, and the faster we can speak to an issue, the less time gossip or false fears can build obstacles in front of our recovery. Immediate, tactful, and truthful communication is an absolute must to build the trust of those around us and to throw out a unifying vision of where we want to end up.

From a cockpit, the COMMUNICATE phase is my opportunity to get other aircraft, air traffic control, and a supervisor of flying who is in place to support our mission on the same radio frequency and tell all of them what has happened, what I've done in response, and where I'm headed. Empowering those other flyers who hear my call, I'll either ask a specific question to fill in what I can't figure out or lay out the blanket, "Okay, what am I missing here?" to all listeners. I am expecting and requiring the help of others to achieve the best possible outcome and now placing an *expectation* on them to help. My bucket of information processing absolutely has a limited capacity.

If you fail to fill in the blanks with what's going on, those without your vantage point, whether senior vice presidents, a mother-in-law, or a roommate, will do it on their own, giving their best guess to help you. And generally, their best guess on your behalf will be unable to hit every target no matter how noble or carefully considered.

Getting hit in the mouth is stunning. It knocks you off balance and makes it awkward to react. There is a second half of a football game I still don't remember after I experienced a head-to-head hit on a kickoff (don't mention this to my flight surgeon). Confusion is sure to follow after getting hit with the Ugly. Acknowledging that what has happened has been painful, followed by detailing some emergency action steps, are critical first words. I have found that I prefer to make room for flexibility, changes, or updates. As a situation unfolds and we learn more, we'll refine our action steps even as we continue to move forward while accepting some degree of ambiguity. I find prescribing or forecasting these changes bounds our expectations that adaptation is normal and not evidence that we've done something wrong. I have told my kids for years that plans sometimes change. Giving ourselves permission to call audibles and adjust to new information or refine our desired end makes change a refreshing sign of recency and relevance as opposed to a disruption or frightening reflection of tardiness and being reactionary.

The interconnectedness of culture and the significant overlaps of touchpoints that occur within family, work, or social circles are beneficial if we can apply our systems understanding to principles of communication. General Jim "Mad Dog" Mattis's great book, *Call Sign Chaos*, honed a similar message to his innumerable subordinates following four decades of exceptional service.[20] He was so adamant and consistent in the importance of this communication model that many of his team members placed his principles, listed here, on notecards on their desks as a constant reminder.

- Clearly identify *what do I know*, articulating between fact and the occasionally required "best guess" while flagging known blind spots that might be clarified later.
- Determine who needs to know.

Can sharing your information make someone else's job more efficient, give early notice of impending action to a superior, or alter another team's plan or accelerate their efforts toward a goal? Perhaps your communication will also help round up some wisdom and assistance for your needs or fill in some of your remaining blind spots.

If I happen to be driving home and can pick up the kids and efficiently run an errand I know is on my wife's to-do list, I am quick to tell Sarah so there is an efficiency of our efforts, and, as we are connected, there is an obvious mutual benefit. The benefit of cross-functional communication is less obvious to organizations which, having less intimacy than a marriage, struggle to know with whom they are connected and how their knowledge benefits others. Being generous with our ideas of who needs to know now mobilizes information as a unifying and effective asset as opposed to a limited and privileged resource. It also empowers the knowledge of the receiver to filter whether or not the information is of value rather than rely on the best guess of the transmitter.

This leads to our last insight:

- Have I told them?

From the jet, this question asks, Have I actually pushed in the microphone switch and broadcast my information to all who might be impacted by this emergency? In other situations, we might ask ourselves: Did I make the phone call, send the text, or, better yet, walk across the street to speak personally with those who most need to know? If we are entrusted to lead, others are looking at us to point them at the desired end zone while they hope we leave them the freedom to decide on the steps to take to get there.

I spent 2017 preparing my fighter squadron for a combat rotation. World events had us preparing with quite different tactics for very different missions in diverse parts of the world. As we drew closer to our deploymet date, our assigned area of responsibility and training finalized, and our preparations were appropriately specific. Then a high-ranking friend called my office from the Middle East. Although he was multiple echelons above my military rank, he knew there was a pending change, with very little notice, to our assigned location. While that message would reach my unit through official notifications in a few days, he knew intimately the impact this curveball would have on our squadron and that we would cherish every moment available to adjust. He intuitively lived Mattis's principles of determine who needs to know and if I have told them.

THUNDERBOLT TAKEAWAYS

Lessons learned or a formal debrief format, training, and real-world experiences have greater impact on our future performance if we take the time to deconstruct and evaluate our performance through them. These steps toward being at our best following a strong right cross are broad enough to allow for a dad who wonders if his words were too harsh for an adolescent daughter or for a vice president of engineering who wants to sharpen how she communicates with her team. Ask yourself a few key questions:

- Reflecting on a personally challenging situation, how do you think you did?
- What would you do differently?
- What message did others hear?
- How does your inner circle think you did?
- When you encounter an inevitable crisis, how emotionally charged is your reaction?
- Does this reaction cause "collateral damage" to others?
- How long does it take for you to move from reaction to an intelligent or even strategic response that can be implemented efficiently?
- How does your behavior or demeanor change when you've moved from a reaction phase to a response phase?

Rest assured, life's circumstances on this side of heaven will hit each of us in the mouth. They will stagger and confuse us and give us the opportunity to respond and recover, better equipped than we would have been with only smooth waters. Christ went so far as to promise these trials to his disciples: "I have told you these things, so that in me you may have peace. In this world you will have trouble. But take heart! I have overcome the world" (John 16:33 NIV). Training ourselves to expect emotional and confusing reactions following a crisis but then implementing a measured response builds the confidence in us to know that embodying Christ's peace and victory are possible during an emergency. To respond as our Savior is to bring wisdom to chaos, words of clarity in the midst of confusion, and peace during a turbulent storm. Training and consideration can equip us for these scary times.

My soul is encouraged by the honesty of the psalmists who give voice to their fears of being overwhelmed. While confident in our experience, we will find greater confidence in God who generously gives wisdom that surpasses all that we might fathom and is fully present in a day of trouble. "Call on me in the day of trouble; I will deliver you, and you shall glorify me" (Psalm 50:15).

10

MORE COWBELL:
EXCEEDING EXPECTATIONS

"I gotta have more cowbell, baby!"
—Christopher Walken, *Saturday Night Live*

My brother-in-law, when a graduate student at the University of Georgia, once spent an entire night in the parking lot of a Chick-fil-A awaiting a store grand opening. Hoping to earn free sandwiches for a year, Justin spent the evening with those whom renowned business author Ken Blanchard refers to as "radical fans." I have read Blanchard's insights as to how organizations expand customer loyalty and satisfaction to generate, not merely repeat, customers. The best customers, of course, are those unique and cultish raving fans who radically "carry the message" (for free!) of a company and become the thrilled acolytes of a business. These radical customers camp out for a midnight release of a video game or create their own fan clubs with dues and shirts and blogs. They almost incessantly discuss all details of a service, movie series, or product.[21]

All businesses need customers, and how to gain them has become an industry in itself. For example, some business leaders encourage a philosophy of "under-promise, over-deliver" as a "poor man's" effort to conveniently generate customer good will. Blanchard, however, elaborates on how critical it is to exceed expectations in a competitive market where merely satisfied customers retain less brand loyalty. Within an industry, creating a personal touch and successfully exceeding customer expectations, even at significant cost, is a wise investment for long term customer loyalty. Marketing experts estimate that it costs nearly three times the amount of money to create a new customer than it does to retain an existing one. Chick-fil-A is exceptional at providing clean, prompt, and high-quality food service while reminding customers that serving them is "my pleasure." Disney manages to market and sell "happiness" to customers who consider an amusement park or a cruise a once-in-a-lifetime experience. They then become once-a-year repeat customers. Libraries of books and blogs have followed suit, and now something extra is nearly the presumption of many customers as the evangelism for radical fans ensues.

Exceeding expectations and leaving room in our lives for the unexpected provide a great send-off for how cultivating the Good, the Bad, and the Ugly can shape our sense of happiness and purpose.

The appeal of doing something more and building radical fans prompted me to consider how I might create that radical energy and commitment, that brand loyalty, on a personal level with my wife and kids. I certainly want my wife to be a radical fan of me amid the monotonous and sometimes exhausting routines of marriage and child-rearing. I want my kids to find their love and validation from their faith and their parents, not other kids or their favorite app. I don't want my children to be merely satisfied with me as they face peer pressure and approach significant life decisions. I would rather they run to us with excitement and trust at every opportunity, question, or obstacle. An idealized picture I know, but my loved ones deserve the best I can provide, and I hope I can exceed their expectations.

As a military officer and like most employees, I want my boss to know that I deliver work that is unique in its quality and forethought—not in the hopes of sucking up to a supervisor but because excellence is its own reward. In the same light, serving as a leader, I strive for the work I do on behalf of my subordinates to be personal and attentive to their individual preferences and interests. Creating raving fans within our work unit produces motivated and energetic team members. Satisfied employees might cordially meet work requirements whereas raving fans are those empowered teammates who anticipate workplace needs and creatively find new solutions to exceed the expectations of coworkers, supervisors, and customers. Delighted supervisors, customers, employees, or loved ones bring an energy of creativity and team-work that no number of inspirational pictures, lectures, or books can.

The Limo of Whimsy

My fighter squadron jointly purchased a 1989 Cadillac Brougham limousine over a dozen years ago. With no regard for subtlety, it was painted gold as that seemed a color to pair nicely with the sun-faded sky-blue velour interior. Additional modifications included the requisite ear-splitting stereo system, a double fin rear spoiler (because downdraft is critical to the interstate maneuverability of a six-thousand-pound car capable of 53 miles an hour), red rims, large stick-ers depicting our squadron mascot, and a dashboard novelty pole dancer. With dignitary flags mounted at the front of our barge, arriving at any tailgate party, rock concert, ball game, or bar generates great enthusiasm as a crew of loud, slightly inebriated fighter pilots announce their arrival.

While I and my friends have become accustomed to the limo, laugh-ing heads turn wherever we drive. I considered this in how I might simply and cheaply exceed the expectations of my own family and create a special memory for all of us. My wife had planned for our family to attend a small community play at a local church on a warm July evening. I told my two oldest children, Jenna and Jake, to wait by the window in the house while my youngest son Trevor and I discreetly retrieved the limo from a friend's home a few blocks away. As Trevor and I made a high-speed reconnaissance pass of our home, I laid on the loud foghorn as Trevor's blond hair flapped out the window. The kids and mom cackled with laughter as we all climbed aboard the gold freighter and headed for dinner and a play. I pulled the limo right out front of a little restaurant in a busy plaza in our small town. At the time, the limo had a deafening belt squeal that was howling across the plaza. Lurching to a stop and waiting for the wake to subside, I quickly hustled around to starboard to open one of three passenger side doors and allow for the "sailors" to disembark. As the belts squealed and my cackling kids and embarrassed wife disappeared into the restaurant, Scott, a golf buddy of mine, exited the same restaurant and was one of many gawkers of the howling gold spectacle.

"What is this?" Scott said.

"A limo," I replied casually, certain that all good workplaces have such a thing. "We're grabbing some dinner and heading to the play."

"Really?" Scott said. "We're headed to the play. With the Danielsons."

"Uh, okay," I responded. "Well, we've obviously got a little room here. How about I pick you up in half an hour?"

And so, our family fun event evolved into a neighborhood family fun event, gaining momentum, energy, and exceeding expectations along the way. Body heat of the piling of three families into the USS Expectations in July quickly began to heat up the interior. Predictably for a 1980s GM vehicle, the dash is full of switches, levers, and lights that, much like a child's Busy Box, keep curious little hands busy but have no perceivable effect on anything in the immediate environment. The kids and moms began sweating through their cute little outfits.

Arriving at the play, I smoothly skippered the gold beauty under a low ceiling concrete parking garage that led to the church entrance. At this point, the belt screech was rock concert loud and reverberating off the concrete structure. After mooring the vehicle, I again leapt out to allow my sweaty passengers a dignified exit in front of dozens of startled attendees whose faces were pressed against church windows as they desperately searched for some impending attack. My wife sprung from steerage, embarrassed and red-faced, accompanied by the fortissimo belt noise and ducked inside.

Perfect.

Mission complete.

Two loud blasts from the ship's horn and with a smiling wave I eased the rig away from the door. The evening reached a crescendo that exceeded even my own expectations.

Befitting a simple pilot and dad who still uses nicknames and hand gestures, exceeding my family's expectations turned out to be an uncomplicated endeavor. It seemed that this easy gesture had gone a long way in generating fun and excitement for family and their little friends.

The limo has since made multiple reappearances. I had an annual commitment to the community daddy-daughter date night, which allowed for the front door arrival and departure for the girls and dads in their best outfits. We've picked kids up from school and ball games, headed for ice cream, and shuttled several kids in that limo, all at the request of parents whom I had never previously met.

While you may not be so fortunate to have access to a gold painted limo with flags and a rear spoiler, doing something small, unforeseen, and perhaps with some embracing whimsy goes a long way in building raving fans within your circle.

By the way, years later, this same limo jumped over a bon fire, crashed into a farm pond, and was towed out. It was also driven to the A-10 weapons range during which the brakes failed on the highway while I was driving my son. That trip culminated with the limo being strafed to death by an A-10. Then we bought another one, but that's a different story.

The Need for Boundaries

While exceeding expectations will bring delight to family, supervisors, and customers, there does exist a loss of boundaries or sense of sanctuary when our perpetual availability to others and need to always deliver more encroaches on our ability to be at our best for those to whom we mean the most. With the global expanse of mobile platforms, and now writing this from my home amid a near worldwide shelter-in-place response to COVID-19, the workplace has reaped the benefits of our willingness to answer text messages or participate in teleconferences seemingly without limit.

Faith, family, and workplace compartments of our lives are now forced to interweave to where barriers between these are now permeable and the consistency, or inconsistency, of our values and priorities are on clear display. I can't tell subordinates to make time for family and then always respond to a half dozen texts between six and ten in the evening while also assigning work to others. Instructing a child to use pleasant speech while I am overheard ridiculing a coworker or asking a studying adolescent to focus as my multitasking proves I am unable to multi-focus forces me to be more aware of modeling successful disciplines.

As technology enabled collaborative efforts and tele-work continues to mature at a rate accelerated by the 2020 pandemic response, how might personal benefits be recouped while the risks of saturating every space of our lives with so-called opportunities to work become realized dangers? For instance, you can pull away from the home office space and have lunch with a loved one, take a quick run with a neighbor, or decompress after a busy meeting on your own patio. The hours saved from reduced or canceled commuting can unearth hours of time for what you love and what will hone your life skills. You can gain time to read, listen to music, hike, exercise, or plan time for intentional efforts to exceed the expectations (surprise) of your loved ones. Of course, there will be times when a real crisis comes up, and you'll need to interrupt your more leisurely plans. Accepting that I may have to take occasional after-hour calls from home, as work and life become more interwoven, can now be counterbalanced by sharing a morning walk with my wife, taking my son out for lunch on a school day or a twenty-minute afternoon splurge of ice cream or watching some of his favorite YouTube videos. An ability to swiftly adjust from being engaged on a work matter and then being fully present for home life seems a skill of compartmentalization and ongoing challenge. Resisting the urge to check work email prior to a family movie or right before bed might increase initial anxiety or fears of missing out while we are learning to create a fenced off boundary, straining to protect a sacred time or place that outside distractions cannot invade.

Delight of the Unexpected

While exceeding expectations professionally requires more of us and can blur the lines separating work and the rest of life, allowing room for the unexpected invites joy and delight to find room on our calendar.

Prairie grass bounced wildly behind the minivan as I raced across a small stretch of Nebraska highway, having left work too late again to deliver my kids where grandparents expected them. The annual summer festival kicked off with a parade that invited kids to dress up and participate, getting their names read on the loudspeaker as they made the turn near the town square. Frantically speeding along, I hustled the kids to "Hurry up and put your outfits on!" I calculated that we were going to pull in at the exact moment they were supposed to start walking in the parade.

Rounding the corner to the drop off point, I looked over my shoulder to see my son Jake, five-years-old at the time, wearing a tall green-peaked witch's hat that was balanced on his bushy rainbow wig, Groucho Marx glasses, and moustache. Then I saw his underwear: whitey-tighties.

"Jake, what are you doing?!" I exclaimed.

Beaming, Jake announced, "I'm the underwear clown!"

"Jake! Pants. A shirt. Now!"

But the picture we snagged and our cackles of laughter at something small, easy, and delightfully unexpected transformed the moment from something dutiful to a real hoot and joy.

As a leader, providing something unexpected to another can thrill and delight. If a pay raise or promotion happens, that's great, but the greatest effect is when those things are unexpected. I came across some old compact discs—reflective small discs with a hole in the middle that we used to buy from a store. A store was a building made of bricks with windows and things. I knew my secretary would like these discs so I gave them to her at work one morning. No big deal. It was a small and inexpensive personal gesture that communicated I knew of her current interests and reminded her that there is more to this office than merely completing tasks. Creating and allowing room for the unexpected can be the nitrous boost of enthusiasm or encouragement a marriage, workplace team, or friendship needs to elevate it to the next level of performance and fulfillment.

As pressure builds to be evermore efficient, to be perpetually available to every call, email, or text, and as our faith, family, and workplace demands and values continue to intertwine, understanding how to navigate this changing environment is crucial to our happiness and those we love. I'm just a dad, husband, and pilot. I want to build raving fans of the people I love. I want to share in an enthusiasm and energy for life with family, friends, and coworkers. I want to be intentional—doing something on purpose and frequently to build a raving fan base in my circles. I shouldn't promise more than I can deliver, but perhaps I can do something a little more, a little better, and personally tailored that connects with others. Exceeding expectations and creating raving fans is a great strategy to build and enrich our relationships. Doing this over time builds rich lives and most hopefully, points others to life in Christ. Doing this consistently requires initiative and, quite possibly, a gold limo and an underwear clown.

THUNDERBOLT TAKEWAYS

- ✗ Recall an unexpected delight or surprise from your childhood. How did it make you feel?
- ✗ How might you exceed the expectations and create energy and delight for another, such as a coworker, neighbor, or family member?
- ✗ How can you build on the magic of exceeding expectations for greater intimacy, joy, or effectiveness, or to point someone toward Christ?

Workplace norms and expectations continue to shift over what it means to work from home, how to connect deeply with others you never see in person, and what normal now means in this world. I laughed recently as I read about one person who said he could no longer discern if he was working at home or now living at work. As we attempt to take ownership of expectations, here are some practical tips to set a baseline of telework expectations.

- ⟋ Get dressed and be deliberate and diligent about your work hours. Start and stop on time. Surge when necessary but not every day.
- ⟋ Build personal breaks into your schedule. If you don't, you can end up sitting in front of your PC for twelve or more hours. Revive a lunch-hour break from your own home office.
- ⟋ Telecommuters now lose that personal think time and post-work decompression time during their commute. So be sure to build think time into your daily work schedule.
- ⟋ You can get quite good at multitasking, but there is no such thing as multi-focused. You are either all the way into the meeting or not. Decide before you join.

Turn your camera on during teleconferencing periodically. I recommend doing this at the beginning and introductory moments of a call as well as during any interaction or questions. It is much easier to decide when to speak when you can *see* the other person has stopped talking. We do this naturally in-person, so do it when you teleconference too. There is evidence of significant fatigue when being so intensely face-to-face all day, but never connecting is also not a viable option.

- ⟋ Camera exception: If you must eat during the call, turn your camera off. No one wants to see barbecue sauce on your chin.
- ⟋ Be punctual. Start and stop on time and convey that expectation to others.
- ⟋ You need to deliberately plan your communications. Hallway meetings don't happen like they do when you're physically in the building together.
- ⟋ Find a place in your home that is reasonably isolated so you and your participants aren't distracted at inopportune times, and you can specifically walk away from work at times during the day.
- ⟋ Be sure that your work setup is ergonomically healthy for your sitting or standing posture.

- Increase your exercise. Remember, if you work at home, you no longer walk between meetings, etc.
- If you don't commute anymore, you'll need to plan when to make those on-the-way-home errands.
- Be mindful of people being in different time zones. Stay within core times for all parties as much as possible.

Parallel parking the gold limo.

Enroute to the community play.

Jake, the Underwear Clown.

11

MUSTACHED AND BULLETPROOF

"You must look at facts because they look at you."
—Winston Churchill

onsultant work is the art of reframing questions, problems, or data to organizations and teams to compel change—that is, to bring improvement or clarity of a roadmap ahead. I enjoy the few occasions I've had to provide this work or to partner with experts of strategic planning to creatively reframe problem sets to accelerate unique solutions. However, consulting work's impact in the workplace remains mixed. Piles of psychological tests, workplace surveys, and slick signage attempt to reveal and propagate an honorable workplace of noble values and socially responsible productivity. Yet, what we say is important, and what actions we take don't always match. It is often the disparity between shiny motivational signs behind chanted team-building mantras and inevitable business or personnel decisions that indicate a team is in trouble.

I've developed a cheaper and faster way to help individuals or organizations better understand themselves so they can move forward more effectively. When I was in eighth grade, a youth pastor asked me three questions that can fast-forward to the important stuff without the need to write a check to a consulting firm:

- Question #1: What do you spend your money on?
- Question #2: What do you spend most of the time talking about?
- Question #3: Who are your friends/allies?

Perhaps that eighth-grade lesson would have saved some morale-sucking conflict over moustaches and money during my last deployment.

Brigadier General Robin Olds was a larger-than-life fighter pilot. Olds was a heroic triple ace flyer from World War II to Vietnam, an all-American West Point football player, and the husband to a Hollywood starlet. General Olds was the embodiment of the warrior hero in a flight suit before the 1986 movie *Top Gun* awakened my generation to fighter pilot culture. General Olds knew how to win, and he thirsted after victory while inspiring and driving teams of acolytes committed to him and the mission of the day. Olds himself lived out his career often running roughshod over any policies, bureaucracies, or leaders who were little more than parasitic drags to his soaring efforts to kill and defeat an enemy.

You don't become the godfather of generations of fighter pilots without whacking a few neighboring rivalries or entrenched power structures. I doubt Olds prepared a multicolor tabbed, labeled, and laminated binder announcing a complex strategic plan to every decision he was going to make as a combat commander for the 8th Tactical Fighter Wing (TFW) in Thailand. But his intentionally disruptive approach broke the thumbs of every sacred yet ineffective office and process of the underperforming 8th TFW. Support systems, slowed or rigid procedures, schedules, manpower alignment, and flight leadership decisions were simply and rapidly sorted by asking: "Does this make us more lethal to our enemies? Does it improve how I keep my people safe?" If the answer to either of those questions was no, then a kneecap whack of realignment was in the making. Even well-intentioned policies or programs that had been handed down and become entrenched parts of a culture, if deemed an unnecessary drag on energy that could be directed to becoming more lethal or more safe, would be discontinued or ignored.

General Olds's legendary status as a fierce combat leader was also advanced by an epic, world-class mustache groomed well outside approved regulations of the time. Marking his individuality, the mustache also enhanced his gunslinger swagger and sparked a wave of followers then and now who claim the mustache made Olds bulletproof. Olds himself viewed the mustache as "the middle finger I couldn't raise in PR photographs. It became the silent last word in the verbal battles . . . with headquarters on rules, targets, and fighting the war."[22] Olds had a long history of breaking rules as well as aggressively leading from the front—the latter a hallmark of effective leadership. His downrange persona wasn't a break from who he was but rather the fulfillment of all he had invested in his career and professional development.

To this day combat deployers are obliged to grow a mustache, routinely beyond regulations, as a uniting sacrament of morale and hope to capture both the bravado and, more importantly, the absolute combat effects of General Olds. The air force has actually endorsed "Mustache March" across the service, dovetailing years-long traditions of fighter squadrons growing mustaches for the month as part of a strange mix of bragging rights and occasional fundraiser to determine the one-month winner. Remarkably, the air force has even recently relaxed the mustache grooming standards ever so slightly as a nod and compliment to the tradition.

I'm not above making poor decisions in my life. My commitment to the fighter pilot culture dictated that I keep the gross lip sweater through a few public speaking events, on camera interviews, and even while officiating my son's baptism. I'm not sure why we haven't framed any of those baptism pictures. Gratefully, I have a patient wife who understands the importance of these uncompromised cultural commitments. At least, I think she tolerates them.

Deployed work trucks get mustaches designed on the nose, and we hang a large metal mustache out the squadron windows for the month of March. We even had a few guys hoist a large picture of a mustache from the back row of a nationally televised morning show broadcast from Bagram.

I've never been prouder of the wit of my unit. I can humbly grow a decent mustache, which is to say it's gross and can seem outsized for my small frame. However, while others cheated by dying their mustaches black for more dramatic effect, I was relegated to runner-up for "Creepiest Mustache" following my last participation. I would argue that our anonymous banana-republic-type balloting had been corrupted by a couple of queasy stomached ladies in the office.

A few years ago, I had the opportunity to lead a combat deployment as a fighter squadron commander. Our squadron had spent the better part of a year preparing for the deployment, adjusting training plans and tactics to an ever-shifting potential location based on global hot spots around the globe and featured in endless news cycles. I took over the squadron and was informed we would be deploying and returning the awesome capability of the A-10 to Kandahar, Afghansitan. This was a location that many of my team had supported in years previous but not one we had specifically prepared for and not to an airfield that currently had any fighter presence. Ironically, I had flown the last A-10 out of Kandahar in 2012, a time when over thirty thousand troops were on base supporting the mission surge at the time. The 2018 change of assignment to Kandahar was to provide close air support firepower to the highly publicized First SFAB (Security Forces Assistance Brigade) deployment to Afghanistan.

When we arrived at Kandahar, the airfield authority had previously been ceded to the army, and previous facilities, dormitories, operations facilities, and communications infrastructure were no longer available to us. The flying mission and personnel footprint had drawn down to a fraction of its previous size. The Kandahar assigned air force support personnel worked tirelessly to prepare for our arrival. Flying in as a twelve-jet whirlwind, our maintenance team had jets armed and combat ready for me to lead the first mission less than twenty-two hours after our arrival.

Deploying military reservists to a combat zone is often an administrative nightmare as long outdated pay systems, order writing programs, legal deployment authorities, and logistic coding parameters lack the fluidity to make rapid changes. Downrange, the squadron quickly ramped up to flying twenty-four-hour operations, immediately employing weapons on the enemy, rearming aircraft, and sending the next pair of A-10s into the air. While busily cutting our own furniture out of plywood and arm-wrestling army inhabitants out of much needed hangar space, we managed to rapidly establish a busy but quality battle rhythm of combat effectiveness. I enjoyed giving out our self-made, biweekly awards entitled the 303rd Fighter Squadron Throat Punch Posse. These awards went to the high performers on our hardworking team. Tired and proud airmen would walk up to thunderous applause from their appreciative coworkers as I gave each one a certificate and a small token of Afghanistan. Afterwards, I gathered with the award winners to pose for pictures. Sporting an ever thickening and slightly illegal mustache at the time, I've never seen anyone have those pictures posted in their work center. Strange.

While first-time deployer Shiner attempted to nurse some transparent peach fuzz into a mustache, grizzled veterans Ponch and Buster magically sprouted cartoonish push-broom mustaches seemingly within moments of landing in the combat zone. Even the female leaders of the KC-135 tanker detachment and rescue helicopter squadrons occasionally sported black mustache stickers for pictures, wore mustache patches on their flight suits, and put mustache-inspired nose art on the noses of helicopters.

Our comradery and sense of pride was built by overcoming obstacles, big and small. But one obstacle arose that we didn't expect. We found out a few weeks into our deployment that well over a dozen of our members were not going to be paid on time for the month and even more members had not received the health benefit entitlements earned while deployed. Twenty-year military veterans had spouses turned away from long awaited specialty medical appointments due to administrative errors and having no record of medical insurance. While the combat requirements continued to hum along, I and our leaders back home jumped into damage control mode, interviewing each affected member, attempting to get banks, credit unions, car loans, or cell phone payments postponed for those airmen who were going to feel the pinch the most. While certainly not due to malicious intent from the air force and a function of the complexity of our pay and orders systems, the deployed members had felt a significant loss of trust. They were deployed to a combat zone on behalf of their nation, generating round-the-clock combat sorties amid frequent rocket attacks on the base, and now they had to cope with how life for loved ones back home had just become more complicated and unnecessarily so. The connectedness of the deployed team members caused others to begin to pick up their own anger and frustration on behalf of their brothers and sisters who had to deal with the headache.

My group commander for the deployment was a great leader and had tolerated, even enjoyed, some of the fighter squadron hijinks and swagger brought to the base. Certainly, his subordinate group and squadron leaders shared in the pride of seeing their efforts recognized in the international press as well as in the daily weapons employment videos provided from our squadron. Chief Crown (not his real name), however, didn't seem as pleased with our arrival. The senior enlisted member of the base generally portrayed a positive outlook but often seemed detached and annoyed by the disruption brought by the round-the-clock mission and members of the fighter squadron. I had noted that while the commander himself was empathetic to the fiscal challenges faced by my troops, even if not equipped to expedite pay corrections, he had at least asked what support he could provide. It seemed that Chief Crown hadn't the time or initiative to get in the trenches with my affected members and provide supportive efforts or encouragement following the pay and insurance debacle that had been quite a blow to our unit's morale.

A few weeks after the dust of our pay debacle had settled, although the pay corrections themselves were ongoing, Chief Crown decided to confront two of my pilots enroute to lunch. To the chief's defense, my guys had spray-painted a squadron stencil on a number of hail-damaged rental cars that we used to drive around base. The stenciling was a long-honored fighter squadron tradition that had never been well received by base leadership over my two decades of combat deployments. Seemingly powerless to make decisions against this inertia, my guys had once again stenciled our assigned vehicles while sporting mustaches that bounced off the regulation limits. One of Chief Crown's peers from a nearby base had also reached out to report that he had overheard some of my pilots bragging about their mustaches. Although I had hosted Chief Crown's peer for a day and half, he never complimented our lethal employment tactics and successful combat effects nor reported his complaint to me at a time and level in which I might have made a correction.

In the end, Chief Crown chose to confront two pilots who had just flown a combat sortie that had begun with a 4:40 a.m. wake-up. The majority of their day had been consumed with the trauma of the fog and friction of war. There had been some initial confusion across controlling and targeting agencies that these pilots may have caused civilian casualties during their mission. Very few things in life can bring terror and rattle a combat aviator's confidence as hearing that your Herculean efforts may have resulted in tragedy. Fortunately, their actions, while lethal, turned out to be accurate, so no civilian casualties had actually occurred. Still, my guys were exhausted and shaken from the day's events. Chief Crown, without adhering to our own formal customs and courtesies while approaching my pilots, photographed the stenciled vehicle and pilots and decided to launch an impromptu interrogation. The retelling, of course, made it back to me, my group commander, and multiple other ears itching to hear and gossip about problems.

A key takeaway from organizational studies and the case study Chief Crown provided is how data compilation reflects actual, not the published or espoused, organizational values and priorities. How a company spends its money, how a group arbitrarily enforces a selection of their existing standards, and what a team spends the majority of their time talking about can paint the clearest picture of organizational values. Beyond the numbers, there is well documented evidence demonstrating that personal and organizational inertia remains undisturbed within a status quo and that it functions solely within familiar and comfortable strengths.

A fascinating insight that professors and business authors Bolman and Deal convey is that organizations love to solve problems they *want* to solve. Note that the authors don't say organizations solve the most important problems or the most fatal problems. Rather, organizations confront the problems they *want* to, which may not be the ones they need to. These problems tend to be ones that had been solved before, problems that look familiar, or problems that bring a sense of accomplishment when fixed by some time-worn solution. This is not only the way organizations typically operate; it's also familiar ground for families and individuals. We gravitate to what's comfortable, even when it comes to handling problems.

Leadership authors such as Collins, Blanchard, Yukle, Bolman, and Deal each warn, in their own language, of the danger of avoiding the brutal facts of reality and, lacking imaginative solutions, becoming complacent with previous successes or processes. These authors advocate for the critical courage to seek out the reality of data, unvarnished and not softened for the eyes of senior leaders. As Collins cites from an interview, "When you turn over the rocks and look at all the squiggly things underneath, you can either put the rock down or you can say, 'My job is to turn over rocks and look at the squiggly things,' even if what you see can scare . . . you."[23] To achieve organizational viability, we need to encourage the development of a corporate culture that is hostile to complacency. Likewise, when it comes to each of us on a personal level, we need to exercise the humility and wisdom to see ourselves and our situations as they really are: the good, the bad, and the ugly. Whether corporately or personally, we will not grow unless we first acknowledge reality, which includes facing the systemic or fatal problems we need to address.

Of paramount need to developing an organizational culture or personal tenant that seeks unflinching facts is actively seeking out and empowering those who can constructively discover and address critical faults, who are courageous enough to tactfully deliver bad news amid the complicated cross-functional chocolate messes in which many teams orbit. Even cocky fighter pilots trying to evoke their inner Robin Olds recognize the critical need to drill down to truth, to data, to the facts in their pursuit of excellence.

Chief Crown could have walked into my office in Kandahar amid the mission planning and self-scrutiny of combat decision making and weapons employment and said, "Your fighter squadron is out of regulations based on their mustaches, and they shouldn't have painted rental cars." If he had done this, I would have recognized that he was completely, factually accurate. Additionally, I do not fault him for being aware of these matters. However, as a key organizational leader, he miserably elected to involve himself and "fix" what was an easy issue to address and a low-level problem he *wanted* to solve. He chose to work a problem that required no independent critical thought, no emotional investment in his fellow airmen, and no creative problem-solving. Worse, Chief Crown chose to reduce his level of leadership and influence, not to matters that cared for the felt needs of countless workers making the mission happen and without pay, but to a few fighter pilots whose swagger had predictably colored outside the prescribed lines. As a leader, Chief Crown's pitch into the fight trivialized and distracted from the more noble decisions that required great effort and focus from each of our team members every day to win. My people needed paychecks and partnership, but instead they were given grooming tips.

So who among us is Chief Crown? I am. Not always. Not every day and not in all situations. But there are blind spots or self-preserving shortcuts that blunt my faith, leadership, and growth as a husband, father, Christian, or leader. I'm human and fallible and prefer to protect myself by thinking I'm courageously confronting the lethal dragons that others ignore. Just as it is easier for organizations to avoid the difficult work of transformative change and substantive improvement, we are individually drawn, like electricity, to a path of least resistance.

I am of Scottish stock, with thick thighs, a barrel chest, and legs barely long enough to reach the rudder pedals in the A-10 cockpit. A towering specimen at five feet, five inches, I am built with a low center of gravity that is ideal for lifting and clearing stones from a moor. At least, I imagine so. Alternatively, I am now a late forties man forced to shop for husky-size pants in the kids section while also unable to run any distance longer than 6 to 9 feet. I'm naturally drawn to sports or conditioning that favors my strengths, such as short sprints, explosive bursts (although less "explosive" and more "plodding" the older I get). I continue to prefer weight training, surfing, or golf for distance, while my fitness score data clearly shows I should focus on improving my one-and-a-half mile run performance. Data-driven decision making would tell me to get on the track and do some running to increase my strength and endurance. But I would rather engage matters that ask less of me. My fitness is an easy and benign example that doesn't require much depth of vulnerability, imagination, or introspection. There are more critical focus areas than looking at my mustache or a one-and-half-mile run time.

I am certain Chief Crown acted without malicious intent, but he did demonstrate a personal and organizational disposition to less risk, tension, and pain. He conveniently interpreted events in known and deeply grooved ruts of familiarity—a nearly universal tendency that devolves problem-solving to the ruts of habit and assumptions and avoids the higher calling of imagination, discernment, and wisdom.

So where might wisdom enter the arena of personal and organizational introspection? I have been blessed to work with some of the smartest and most talented fighter pilots, microchip engineers, special tactics soldiers, C-suite executive leaders, speakers, and authors that America has to offer. Even among this group, there appears a divide from those whose progression stops at smart and those whose emotional maturity forms a foundation for wisdom. The book of Matthew quotes Christ in the sermon on the mount. Jesus tells his followers in 5:13, "You are the salt of the earth." And in verse 14, "You are the light of the world." Salt and light were powerful metaphors for that time, and they can still guide us today. Salt is a most valuable resource that enriches flavors, a preservative that allows something to endure, and a disinfectant to clean what's dirty. To be light is to provide something bold and able to draw and guide others as well as reveal anything hidden. Simply spoken, can we take steps to be like salt and make everyone around us better? Can we be as light, able to discover or reveal something difficult to see while also guiding a vision or direction for a team to follow? Certainly steps can be taken to help us focus on making others better, on caring and inspiring others in a manner that aligns personal as well as organizational goals.

As I pursue wisdom, trying to avoid blind spots and committing to never prioritize facial hair over personnel well-being, I've adapted some things I've learned from a collection of incredible leaders, pastors, teachers, and coaches.

As a young lieutinent, I remember briefing a mission with a decorated A-10 pilot who had suffered as a POW during Desert Storm. His call sign is "Sweetness," and he is an A-10 and fighter aviation legend with impressive skills and experience. I felt more of a tag-along nuisance to him than a combat-ready wingman able to provide mutual support. This feeling began to go away when he finished his pre-mission brief by looking at me and saying, "Okay, what did I miss?" This simple, short, and humble invitation to partner together gave little Scottish-bodied me permission to help him get better. Rather than praying for perfection and worrying my mistakes would dominate my flight lead's thoughts during the post-mission debrief, the war hero I was flying with talked about his mistakes and chuckled at my "insights" and confessions. Together, we moved forward.

Smart people surround us. But it's not enough to be near them or to have them on the team. You must empower them to answer, "What did I miss?" It's often disarming for others when we humbly point out our own mistakes and misperceptions. Building that trust by modeling vulnerability invites the feedback and varied frames of interpretation we desperately need for avoiding blind spots. I would occasionally take this a step further. I would encourage a wingman to know that we were on the same team to accomplish the mission that day and that he had specific important roles. One of those roles was to use his mind to keep us out of trouble. I would then assure him that I was ultimately responsible for the day, but if I made a mistake that my wingman could have helped me avoid and didn't say anything, I might be the one with negative paperwork, but he would be the one washing my car for a year. We need to speak up, and we need those around us to do the same. Otherwise, we may miss something important.

I don't prefer conflict, but I don't typically run away from it either. Conflict is inevitable, and my default position is that I'm going to find a way to win. Not exactly an approach that builds either partnership or understanding. It's always a short-sighted win when we strive just to win an argument or engage in quick verbal sparring while failing to build on the mutual understanding of why we may be locked in different positions. When addressing conflict, my younger impulse would see an obvious answer and, with barbs attached, spear the opponent with a fury of logic and snark that displayed no patience for a counter explanation. My dad taught me a simple approach to ease potential conflict and temper my impatience with those who failed to immediately embrace my most recent epiphany of "brilliance" or change implementation. My dad's phraseology went something like this: "Help me understand _____" (fill in the blank).

- "Help me understand why we seem reluctant to speak to each member who hasn't been paid."
- "Help me understand why we execute this step of the process."
- "Help me understand why we seem reluctant to implement our plan."

Inviting others to teach through their thoughts respects another's position while allowing and urging them to make clear their rationale. Also, when asking for help, the questioner helps to reduce any power distance or competitive tension by beginning in the "need" position.

Lastly, invite an Otto into the room of your decision makers. Otto was a former East German pilot that I flew with as a T-38 instructor pilot in Texas. Otto was loud and brash. He spoke with broken English and was confrontational. He was a challenge to lead, not a favorite among the other students, and could derail any instructor meeting. He was also uniquely correct and properly challenging at least 40 percent of the time. Finding a way to win with him on the team involved constant adjustments. And, to be forthright, I was dismissive of him even when he was correct. It took the honesty of another Dutch pilot to open my eyes to Otto's value. Otto had found his way to my group of students and instructors I commanded. He had proven too difficult in his previous home. I was lamenting my weariness and recalling a recent disagreement with Otto to my trusted assistant commander. He looked at me and said, "Otto is right." I was properly humbled. I finally realized that I needed to find a way to glean Otto's 40 percent of valuable inputs without losing my mind in the process and then have the courage to act on them, even if they were not the problems I wanted to solve.

My hopes amid conflict are slowly maturing from winning or gaining a quick kill to conveying a defensible rationale. I would prefer to persuade or influence another person to adopt my position, but often disagreements remain. However, I now know to look for people like Otto in the room who are far more likely to show me personal blind spots in my decision roadmap as I'm also forced to speak through my own position, providing my reasoning and what I am valuing in the end.

When General Olds returned from Vietnam, upon direct confrontation, he shaved the mustache that had brought energy to a wing that had become complacent and ineffective. My mustache was shaved within moments of arriving home, partly because the deployment was over but also because a razor waited on the front porch of my house before my beautiful wife would let me come in. Olds and his mustache inspired mine and thousands others half a century later. He provided the thunderbolt-like message to all he encountered: "Let's win by keeping the most important things first."

During seasons of intensity, when data and an onslaught of decisions amid competing organizations begin to dilute our clarity of values and missions, we may need a thunderbolt strike to refocus our purpose each day. Our goals or missions must always strive to meet the highest calling of integrating the needs of people with the demands of the organization. As leaders, we need to pursue on both personal and organizational levels the roles of salt and light. We must look to enrich those around us, to accentuate their strengths, to preserve and value them while having the courage to illuminate or expose core problems as we also cast a well-lit vision for what is ahead.

THUNDERBOLT TAKEAWAYS

To evict the Chief Crown taking up residence in my own heart which naturally prefers to remain detached and find the easiest, most rehearsed answers, I invite a few techniques:

- ✒ Are we passionately directing our focus and energies toward the most critical of mission needs?

It is essential personally and professionally to distinguish between what's critical for our mission or life success from that which is secondary in importance or a weighty distraction.

✗ Am I providing both public and private recognition for the sacrifices, commitment, and performance of others?

Whether for family, coworkers, or subordinates, this recognition is super appreciated and reinforcing while the absence of recognition or a dismissive presumption of excellence diminishes a team's cohesion and commitment.

✗ Welcome an Otto into our life.

We each have a self-protective bias that makes ignoring problems feel safe and convenient. Even if a style is difficult, who is your Otto? Who could it become? How can you nurture that relationship and make a direct appeal for that person's input?

✗ Ask "What did I miss?"

To make power distance short and to routinely invite a humble and teachable spirit, ask this question of those around you—often. Empower others to help you see the squiggly things of realism in our lives and embrace those truths while growing a posture of humble learning.

✗ When confused and unsure of how to respond or even when anticipating a disagreement, rehearse the phrase "Help me understand . . ."

Invite others to teach. Intimately understanding the views of others and building consensus are critical to building a high performing team. If we are wise enough to take a strategy for the long win, we must invite others to teach their position, to help us understand their perceptions and context, realizing all along that we need to subject our own rationale to significant scrutiny as our turn to teach will shortly follow.

We need to be challenged, and we need to follow the data and be held accountable for fulfilling the team values. And lastly, if ever in doubt, policy— whether it deals with facial hair or anything else—should never make us dumber or be our shortcut to avoiding the hard work of solving messy problems.

Deployed fighter squadron commander, complete with requisite Olds inspired bad mustache. Standing in front of Tail #093, my hail-storm tail from 2000 and later my commander's jet from 2017-2019. (Chad Garland / © 2018 Stars and Stripes, all rights reserved)

With 451 AEG/CC, Colonel "Joker" Jones, the deployed group commander at Kandahar Air Base, Afghanistan. (Chad Garland / © 2018 Stars and Stripes, all rights reserved)

Reuniting with family following a deployment is one
of my favorite memories. This photo was taken only
moments before the family violently required
that my combat mustache be shaved.

Home Sweet Home

12

ACTUALLY

"But as for you, you meant evil against me;
but God meant it for good."
—Genesis 50:20 NKJV

"I was one way and now I'm completely different.
And the thing that happened in between . . . was Him."
—Mary Magdalen, *The Chosen* TV series

A former commander of mine told me a story of a great measure of friendship. If you ever find yourself on the wrong side of the law in the middle of the night and in jail and you are able to call a friend, a friend will tell you that he will pick you up first thing in the morning. A *good* friend, however, will tell you he is coming to you straightaway. Your *best* friend, however, will turn and look you in the eye and say, "Man, that was fun!"

The apostle Paul was imprisoned and, I suspect, had a curious optimism reserved only for those able to annoy you, like a best friend. Paul was writing a letter to Christians in Philippi, many of whom were generous friends deeply grieved and distressed by his wrongful imprisonment. In the opening lines of his letter, he is no disassociated Pollyanna presuming everything will work by ignoring his circumstance. He leaves the negative facts in place: he has been persecuted, he's in chains, and he remains under Roman guard. Other highlights include being shipwrecked, stoned, and bitten by a viper. Writing to his friends at Philippi to thank them for their love and gifts, Paul addresses their concerns for him: "I want you to know, beloved, that what has happened to me has *actually* helped to spread the gospel" (Philippians 1:12, italics added). *Actually*, from the Greek word *mallon*, conveys "really served" or "rather, instead of." Paul says "actually" to pivot the entire narrative of his persecution to a broader reality regarding ongoing purpose and progress. *Actually* means that Paul can now see God's sovereignty, weaved into the events the Romans had intended for evil, as having advanced the cause of Christ. In addition to emboldening other Christians amid persecution, Paul says that all of the guards of Caesar's palace knew of him and that he was imprisoned due to his faith amid constant threat. His imprisonment was an effective witness to approximately four thousand five hundred Praetorian guards. Those he was writing to struggled to understand the power of actually and how that word can reframe our entire understanding of circumstances, suffering, success, and purpose.[24]

During our last academic year at Nebraska, my wife was finishing her undergraduate work in speech pathology while I was serving as a youth pastor and taking a few graduate classes. I had received word nearly a year in advance that I was chosen for pilot training in Texas, and each day was seemingly a countdown to getting commissioned and heading off to fly jets. I was chasing being a fighter pilot, pulling Gs, and playing volleyball without a shirt. (Just kidding about the volleyball. The original 1986 movie *Top Gun* featured volleyball; the scene was replayed with beach football for the 2022 sequel, *Top Gun: Maverick*.) I was ready to do all the exciting things that music videos and Hollywood featured.

We unloaded our Ryder moving truck in Wichita Falls, Texas, on the first of what became thirty consecutive days over 100 degrees. A difficult welcome. Arriving in early July, my assigned training class didn't start until nearly a year later due to the number of students in the pipeline. I wasn't going to fly until nearly two years after I knew of my selection. This seemed an eternity to me as I had been directing my life to this opportunity since seventh grade.

I was assigned to the Department of Reports and Analysis (DORA) at Sheppard Air Force Base where I was tasked with typing in the names and sortie hours of the hundreds of pilot trainees flying jets ahead of me. I've never seen any movie trailers blending a year of data entry in a shared cubicle with soaring guitar riffs and jets streaming wingtip vortices across blue skies. I sat forty hours a week and did data entry. I would occasionally escape to the link-trainer room (imagine instrument and gauges used only for flying practice but with no visuals) and practice ground checks. I imagined, surely, I would slip into some class a little earlier than where I had been scheduled. I routinely welcomed new pilot trainees, helping them find their way around base, teaching them which Mexican food places to avoid, and getting them in-processed. And I burned with youthful frustration and envy as they launched into training coursework within days of their arrival. My misery hung on me like a bad odor.

The time in DORA allowed me an informal head start studying the T-37 "Tweet" operational limits numbers of engines and hydraulic systems and practicing ground operations. I had no real flying experience and was still unaccustomed to a high-pressure military training environment. But at the time, I was a fool who failed to cherish the momentary lighter workload and chance to prepare. Instead, I grumbled about how I should have received an earlier training class and how data entry could possibly be the world's worst use of my obviously formidable skills.

Through the lens of hindsight, however, I can see how important this time was for my wife and me. Sarah was able to enroll and complete her masters in speech-language pathology and audiology. Had we not been in Wichita Falls for at least two years, it is unlikely she would have finished the professional degree that she loves and is blessed to use to this day. For me, I'm not sure I would have earned my wings or performed at a level to deserve an A-10 had I not had that time to get somewhat accustomed to the intense training environment and flying world prior to my class date. I still got nervous driving up to the gate for my first month as a lieutenant. I certainly wasn't ready to learn something in a 120-degree cockpit in an inverted spin with an angry NATO instructor candidly debriefing my every inadequacy. That season of life required some significant maturing, becoming intimately familiar with scrutiny, failure, and grit.

During my first month of flying, I threw up a few times in my mask, which life support was forced to bag and throw away. I was counseled both times that a green apple and two Snickers bars were an inadequate preflight meal. I remember being a little slow to respond to my instructor once, and he looked down between high area spin sets and noticed my oxygen hose had come unplugged. My labored breathing and mild hypoxia weren't clues to me that something was wrong. I was often initially confused as to what my angry instructor was saying, so the conditions didn't seem that different. Captain Merry (ironic actual name) had some good Friday night stories to tell following that event. I would say it was embarrassing, but I don't remember most of it—one of the advantages of hypoxia, I suppose.

I did my solo flight on time, but I also forgot to put my gear down prior to cracking my wings in the final turn. The gear finally came down, of course, but I was forced to carry a used tire around the flight room as a friendly reminder of proper procedure. The solo flight was an epic accomplishment to us aspiring students. We celebrated it by throwing one another into a cattle tank painted with our class logo with water forbidden to ever be changed.

Most things in life had generally come easily to that point. But initial flying was not included on that list. All of those years turned out to be critical ones. They provided a foundation for empathy, focus, and performance as a fighter pilot and instructor. Those years and the ones that followed have also grown me in all of my roles as husband, dad, officer, and fighter pilot. Each role has helped me become better at the other ones.

One of my favorite things to do in a jet is fly at 100 feet above ground level amid the saddles of hills and mountain valleys, be they in Alaska, Arizona, or the rolling limestone terrain of Missouri. At 100 feet, even at the pedestrian speeds of the A-10 of about 5 miles a minute, there is little time to focus on anything other than what is in the next one minute in front of you. Birds, trees, cliffs, towers—low altitude flying is amazing fun and a critical skill for threat evasion. Oftentimes, following a low altitude attack or navigation training, we'll practice a route abort exercise, pulling back aggressively on the stick, standing the jet on its tail, and soaring out of the low altitude structure. Within moments you are more than a mile above the earth and now privileged to an entirely different perspective than what you had seen mere seconds previously.

Only in hindsight can I see the countless times when I was so engrossed in the intensity of the next minute of life, the next saddle or set of rocks, that the inevitable disappointments or offending moments of life were only magnified because of the narrow perspective I had at the time. Perhaps you follow a similar pattern of frustration or disappointment or loss of motivation and questioning when a project, opportunity, or relationship miserably implodes. Those moments, and hopefully they are rare, are occasions that I wish I had the perspective of Paul. I wish I could rip back on the stick and climb up out of the valley and take a look at where I'm headed and see the purpose, perhaps a disaster averted, that God's sovereignty has orchestrated. I'm not sure when the Lord brought some perspective to my mind. I remember asking my wife to forgive me years later. Certainly the Lord saw past my grumbling and blessed us with my wings, Sarah's degree, and some much-needed seasoning for the years ahead.

I remain a work in progress. I continue to search out ways to dampen the amplitude of hurt or anger when the occasional injustice or irrational or unfair touches me or my family. I want to be able to sit in the middle of the jail cell with Paul, even if feeling pain or sadness while shackled, and be able to say, "*Actually*, the Lord is slowly revealing a greater purpose." Perhaps a different avenue, a greater outcome, an investment in my character, or a boldness and authentic confidence that is only able to mature when overcoming difficulty—these form the deeper story, the one far more significant than the circumstances. I need to breathe and believe that *actually* has a role in my journey of faith.

When encountering crises—perhaps small ones that seem big to the small people in your house, or perhaps significant life-altering shipwrecks to you, a loved one, or a coworker—is *actually* and its power anywhere in your vocabulary? Reflecting on various difficult seasons, stolen opportunities, or bias, are you able to make room for the word *actually* into the story that pivots your paradigm and allows for positive growth for you or others in the story? Positive memories of special moments in marriage or finding good takeaways from challenging seasons of life are hallmarks of resilient and joyful hearts. Like Paul, we don't need to edit out the negative facts or think that denial and avoidance are great coping mechanisms. But if the only thing that comes to our hearts and minds are raw emotions and ruminations of how we've been wronged or were miserable, those are the patterns of thought that allow bitterness to move to the forefront of our presence, joining hands with cynicism and permeating through our parenting, faith, marriage, and workplace. Our world needs us to be better.

Making room for *actually* also means that you are inviting a richer perspective about life that is likely to counter that of your friends and colleagues who remind you that you deserve to be angry. If you're seeking wisdom or a reason to persevere, attempting to rocket out of the narrow canyon floor and look over the wing to gain some perspective on what's ahead, you may be surrounded by others who lack the wisdom to pursue that point of reference. Churning over gossip and bad news, political rivalries, or how "the man" is holding us down are strangely where some people come alive and prefer to dwell. It even seems better to this type to attempt to launch some counterattack of retribution. Inviting the Lord's presence to shape our heart through hardship when every emotion or fiber of your soul is hurting is not a natural or intuitive response. It is a difficult and starkly countercultural choice. It's a choice that simply makes room in our mind's eye for a glimpse of hope or meaning, however briefly, around the next mountain of the low altitude run. We may not see all the way to the end. Perhaps we are protected from a view all the way to a finish, but for this season, we're looking for reassurance that we're not lost or forgotten, and we need fresh energy to push ahead. For me, this choice starts with a conversation with God. "Lord, I don't understand. This seemed a wonderful fit for me and my family. I'm hurt and angry." Or, "Lord, this terrible prognosis or revelation has just landed on our doorstep. I have no idea what you are doing. Help us to honor you and make wise decisions in the weeks ahead. Help us to still love even if we never fully understand why us."

We also need to find some ability to distance ourselves from the intensity of what we may be experiencing. I imagine this is like trying to see a clear reflection of yourself while positioned only one inch away from a mirror. We need to seek wise counsel and saturate ourselves in the wisdom and perspective of Scripture to gain enough distance from the mirror to determine how we are reacting. *Am I moving forward?* Equally important, *Can I, like Paul, see beyond myself and adjust my focus to others? Am I making things worse for those around me?*

We don't know how long Paul waited before he was able to experience a pivot amid his pain to a persevering strength that was fueled by a greater vision of what his experience was really serving. I am hoping to reduce the amount of time that cycles for me or my family members between anger or misery and pivoting with the assurance that knows the Lord never leaves us, therefore he is at work. Somehow. Even though I may not like the situation or understand it. I can still trust a Father who sent his Son to die for me. And I don't need to wait years to be at peace with the circumstances or cause mountains of collateral damage in the midst of them.

Actually is a great word to hear Paul use amid his hardship. I would prefer life to never provide a situation to use it myself. I think our culture would prefer *actually* to sound more like abbracadabra, an incantation that magically whisks us out of difficult situations. I know all about whisking. I used to be an instructor pilot in the T-38. Some older guys used to call the jet the white rocket. Developed in the 1950s with a sleek coke-bottle fuselage, when flying on the deck, the little supersonic jet can skoot pretty well and climb like a rocket. We used to ask for a max performance takeoff when the circumstances allowed. We would accelerate in full afterburner, perhaps a little too far off the departure end of the runway to get more smash, and then pull back for a vertical climb soaring through 10,000 feet in seconds.

While exhilarating, this is not how daily life works, not even daily flying. Although we may hope to remain distant and saved from hardship, the reality is that life will likely require us to turn back into the low altitude valley and make our way through the hardship. The power of *actually* is to turn hardship and the impossible to hope. Realizing we serve a role in something bigger than ourselves directly impacts our present lives and circumstances. I am certainly not able to respond as a spiritual giant to every circumstance and that's not a realistic goal anyway. The goal is to invite room for perspective and wisdom that wasn't present before. The more noble and higher the calling, the greater our joy and perseverance for us and our roles.

Inviting *actually* into our lives makes room for richer stories and higher purpose. It also moves us from the hapless victim, a present-day popular role to play, to a compelling character empowered to impact the story around us. I think Paul would look to us and say, "Actually, aim high!"

THUNDERBOLT TAKEAWAYS

- ✔ Is there a conversation you need to have with the Lord about a difficult circumstance?
- ✔ What does that conversation sound like?

Perhaps you can start with simple, honest vulnerability. Here's a possible jump start: "Lord, I don't understand. I'm hurt and angry (or confused, heart-broken, frustrated, frightened, anxious, devastated, wounded . . .) about what has happened."

- ✔ Realize the tension of needing to mesh this honesty without prolonged self-pity and self-absorption. Like the psalmist, we can note God's love and his presence amid the most difficult seasons of life (Psalms 23 and 69).
- ✔ When life feels broken and unjust and confusion abounds, yank back on the stick and ask God to provide a cockpit view, perhaps a mile above your circumstances, that will reassure you of his presence and purpose. This will bring into focus the idea that God is actually doing something more significant and strategic than we understand (Isaiah 55:9).

13

DON'T DO ANYTHING STUPID

"Wounds from a friend can be trusted,
but an enemy multiplies kisses."
—Proverbs 27:6 NIV

"**S**on, don't do anything stupid."

"Dad! You were out at 3 a.m.?!" my son, Jake, said excitedly with wide eyes and a large grin.

He was reading some old newspaper clippings I had gathered from a basement trunk to prepare for a speech. Jake beamed as though this archived evidence was giving him permission to do something just as stupid as his father had done decades ago. But nearly universally, bad decisions make for good stories and eventually teachable illustrations. My hope for my kids is that they accept vicarious learning and can avoid the pains of some of my buffoonery. And to the delight of his ears, I shared a flashback of how I had made some bad decisions.

I sat in the backseat of the police cruiser (which is a good introduction to any story) and glanced up, catching my reflection in the rearview mirror. I looked out from under an absurd Gilligan-style bucket hat upon which I had transferred stickers from my football helmet, and I saw my own disbelieving face as the net from the basketball district championship game a few hours before hung around my neck. My cocky smirk had morphed into a sickened but not quite panicked expression. *Dreams of flying jets might not get out of the chocks with a police record*, I thought.

The officer was looking down in his lap, writing some notes I supposed. The officer looked up into the mirror and our eyes locked. "Not a good night, is it Todd?"

"Woody?" I said, startled.

"I've already called your parents," Officer Woodhead replied as he handed me my "Defendants Copy" of a ticket for trespassing.

Woody was a teammate from church league basketball. We went to church together—my dad's church! And upholding the time-honored tradition of a preacher's kid misbehavior, I was doing my part to find the wrong side of the law. Here's how I ended up in the back of squad car.

My high school senior picture features a red Honda CRX, a football helmet, a dated flop haircut, and a regrettable sweater with teal and purple stripes straight from a 1990s television sitcom. In that setting and as an inconsequential member of our high school basketball team, we won our district championship for the sixth consecutive year and were headed back to the state tournament. I had moved to the school the year prior and wasn't familiar with the traditional post-game festivities of a district championship. I was told to wear black.

Heading out with a teammate, my dad looked down the stairs at me and saw the black clothes, the net hanging around my neck, my bucket hat pulled down over my eyes, and a small pair of wire-rim glasses that glowed in the dark. Pondering the inevitable, my dad said, "Son, don't do anything stupid." With a snort of laughter, I slipped past him as a cocky high school athlete would and told my dad not to worry.

Arriving at the appointed team rendezvous, I was told that our plan for the evening was to uphold the tradition of the previous five championship teams.

As innocent victims of circumstance, we really had no choice but to toilet paper the school courtyard from the surrounding four roofs as our honored predecessors had done. Pooling together our money, we walked out of the Super Saver grocery store after midnight with 492 rolls of toilet paper jammed into shopping carts. We parked a few blocks from the school and made our way onto the roofs surrounding the school courtyard. Teammates helped lower, or more accurately drop, me and the other point guard to the ground in the courtyard. For what seemed like an hour or more, teammates would throw toilet paper over and across the trees and down into the courtyard while my friend and I would throw the rolls back up over the trees and onto the roof to allow for maximum streamer effect. The artistic exuberance was impressive.

Our festivities were interrupted when I heard footsteps racing above, kicking the rocks that lined the roofs. I looked up to see the silhouette of our six-foot, four-inch center scampering across the top of the east building with red and blue lights bouncing off the clouds behind him. I sprinted toward the corner of the courtyard, rejoined with my teammate, and tried to burrow beneath some bushes. "Stop running!" were the calls we heard from the police officers through their megaphones.

My reaction was to hurriedly dig a bigger foxhole and settle in for the night. My game plan was to wait for class to start in five or six hours and look for a basketball fan walking by. I would then knock on the locked door, hoping that a sympathizer would open it and allow me to slip into hallway traffic and off to class with no one the wiser.

Hiding behind the bushes, I looked at my friend, now wearing my glow-in-the-dark glasses. We soon surrendered from our fortified position and were helped up out of the courtyard by a good-humored police officer. Being escorted toward a cruiser, I walked past a teammate who, I think, was handcuffed to the branch of a small tree as I was pointed to the backseat of the car.

As I saw my reflection in the mirror of the squad car, my dad's words inexplicably and miraculously transformed from a trivial paternal worry to, well, wisdom. I connected his words to the lyrics of the inimitable Johnny Cash when he sang about being arrested while wearing black. Perhaps I should have listened to my dad a bit more than Cash.

Anyway, the principle not to do anything stupid resounds for those in the highest levels of global leadership down to those developing teens trying to find their way. Even with the most intense efforts at self-improvement, a militant study of self-actualization, or a committed avoidance of gluten, nothing can deliver a needed bullet of truth to one's heart more accurately than an empowered member of your closest circle. I trust that a journey for refinement and wisdom that's rooted in faith and the truth of Scripture will enrich our lives. I also know that my natural human condition is frail and selfish. We all need trusted advisors in our lives.

The phrase "trusted advisors" elevates from political nicety to critical life support when we realize the prophet Jeremiah's words are true for each of us: "The heart is devious above all else; it is perverse—who can understand it?" (Jeremiah 17:9). This passage isn't a note to paralyze hope, despite being frightfully true. Rather, we are warned of the natural limits of our ability to truly know our intimate motives and to avoid a blind trust in every personal thought or inclination. This vulnerability is why we each have a need (are designed?) for an inner circle. We need to energize those cells closest to us, those people who touch our lives directly, by giving them permission and opportunity to speak truth into our lives—truthful words to help avert disaster, to share in triumphs, to course adjust from a given path, and to embolden our steps on a chosen course of action. Much like the reflection in a mirror, we need an instrument outside of ourselves to help orient our perspective, provide fidelity, and give us a glimpse of what we can't see on our own. There are countless examples of those whose lives, careers, and companies have imploded due to an arrogantly opaque self-reliance.

In a freezing drizzle in March 1841, newly elected US President William Harrison delivered a nearly two-hour inaugural address. Elected president at sixty-eight-years old, the oldest president elected until Ronald Reagan in 1980, he was keenly aware that his age and general poor health created a public perception that he was too feeble to lead the nation. To demonstrate his strength and vitality, President Harrison refused to wear a coat and hat for the inauguration. He also chose to ride on horseback instead of in an enclosed carriage to deliver his speech. Following the lengthy address, Harrison attended three balls still wearing his wet clothes. He subsequently caught a cold and died of pneumonia one month later. Proving the public correct, the president suffered fatal consequences of his inability to self-govern and come to terms with his own frailties. William Henry Harrison demonstrated that even our nation's commander in chief is not immune from disastrously bad decisions.

As I looked at a copy of his speech in the Smithsonian, I wondered if his inner circle was tempted to say anything or if they were even empowered to speak ahead of this disaster. His friend, Daniel Webster, edited the speech but was unsuccessful in getting the length significantly reduced. His wife, Anna, who obviously knew of his poor health, was not in Washington at the time to provide a wise correction and to remind him that he had, in fact, already won the presidency and there was no need for the flamboyant risk. None of us need to suffer Harrison's fatal consequence of choosing to go it alone. We still have the opportunity to nurture a trusted inner circle of truth-tellers.

Healthy, engaged, and energized inner circles rarely happen in the wild without intentional cultivation. When you look in a mirror, you expect to see an exact representation of your appearance. Perhaps you would prefer the mirror was a little less honest at times. If the only reflections we saw were those of funhouse mirrors (I like the one that makes you look taller), we would have a distorted image, a tragically inaccurate image of our actual appearance. In the same way, we benefit the most from an inner circle of those courageous enough to provide an accurate reflection of our condition. It is far safer to surround ourselves with suck-ups—yes men or women or those tepid souls who can cheer us but remain unlikely to challenge us when we need it the most. So, if the adage is true that we are a result and reflection of the five people we allow closest to us, who populates your inner circle?

Vulnerable, authentic leadership, in any capacity, is often the most compelling and endearing manner to draw a team together. To be vulnerable to an audience is a powerful act of placing your motives, strengths, fears, and thoughts, without a self-protecting varnish, before others who can respect that courage and often respond in kind. As a leader, people with whom you develop that kind of relationship will respond with great effort and loyalty. Sharing in such a way with an inner circle will return a properly wise blend of correction and encouragement. I've attempted to fast-forward this intimacy a few times by prescribing the conversation with a friend and forecasting my need to get my ego out of the way.

"Look, I think there's probably a reason I'm wrong here given how mad I am. I'm going to tell you what I'm thinking and why, and I need you to pick it apart for me." This was in Kandahar, Afghanistan. I had no time for hugs and meditative music, and no incense was required to get to what I needed to hear. And he told me, clearly. And I said thank you, expecting my slightly hurt feelings and an urge to justify myself to subside in the hours ahead.

Hopefully your opportunities are in a less intense or desperate situation, but simply prescribing roles and expectations immediately gives you permission to be honest and unburden your soul, removes any superficiality, and has assigned your trusted friend a speaking part in the conversation to follow. As a vulnerable leader, capable of things both great and tragic, you need to initiate these conversations as a routine wellness check and simply ask, "Hey, do I have a blind spot here?" You can't expect life circumstances to magically arrange these encounters.

Choosing whom to award a premium spot in your inner circle is no small matter. I want someone who has the emotional maturity to disagree, perhaps pointedly, and can separate the subject of contention from the forward momentum of our friendship. This doesn't mean you choose an unemotional robot to share with. I simply mean that one can say, like a fighter pilot (perhaps with fewer four-letter words), "That could be the dumbest thing I've heard today. Let's get lunch, and I'll tell you why I really don't think we should do that."

Following the adage of hire slowly and fire quickly, I want to be very selective of the mouthpieces I invite into my life and look for those who are wise, simple to understand, and creative. I am fortunate my wife can fill each of those roles at different times. But there are other occasions and other challenges when we need to hear from different members of our personal executive board who have varied experiences and expertise that might make for a better fit. Regarding firing, cultivating these relationships means that I may need to pull some weeds on occasion and alter to whom I confide and entrust with the role of personal truth-teller. Sometimes circumstances, a new job, a different location, or a different stage of life may drive changes.

As fighter pilots, we're nearly incapable of talking about anything but ourselves or flying, and we often have the strange idea that we, through some interplanetary phenomenon, are now the center of the universe. Although disorienting at first, if I bravely remove myself from the middle of this circle and place others I know in the center, I need to immediately consider their values, their potential journey while chasing a dream, and how I might humbly attempt to help them be at their best.

The obvious puzzle piece left for us is to determine what must be done to be worthy of having an impact and speaking truth into the life of another. Occasionally, an organizational position or job title, such as boss or dad or commander, may obligate my role as a truth-teller in another's life. More powerful than these examples of positional leadership, which is characterized by job performance feedback, is *relational* leadership. Relational leadership is fueled by mutual respect and a treasuring of the wisdom of another—a wisdom and presence which are invited and given a place of honor and influence in the life of another. Relational leadership is earned, not bestowed; it's based on the merits of our character and the depth and quality by which we connect with others.

So how do we become a valued truth-teller for another? James, Jesus's older brother, provides some counsel we can apply to this matter: "You must understand this, my beloved brothers and sisters: let everyone be quick to listen, slow to speak, slow to anger" (James 1:19). There are some critical guidelines to consider in being worthy of the trust placed in you as part of the inner circle of another. One is to control your tongue. It is easy to let words slip that may betray a confidence, to easily agree or accelerate the disparagement of a supervisor rather than come to a defense, or to give full vent to your anger. Being one who is often too quick to speak, I can empathize with the comedian who lamented, "I often find out what I think as I say it." The dangers of a loose tongue are that the damaging fire that we spew from our mouths is impossible to control once lit. Proverbs 12:18 says, "Rash words are like sword thrusts, but the tongue of the wise brings healing." Better to be wise than rash and foolish.

I love a quick wit, and strong opinions are often the engine by which change and improvement come. I would never advocate for a blandness of speech that fails to have meaning or be compelling. Political candidates often fill enough airwaves with that language. Wise speech, however, is capable of both measuring moments of silence as well inserting a well-crafted insight or retort, like a spice that enriches a meal, holding the power to alter a conversation or even the heart to whom we speak. Passionate or forceful speech can have its occasional place in our lives if those measured words are driven by a humble and constructive intent and not merely a reactionary, inflammatory, or destructive diatribe. I think Scripture provides the best principles of how we are to speak. "Let your speech always be gracious, seasoned with salt, so that you may know how you ought to answer everyone" (Colossians 4:6).

Although managerial books trumpet the need to be a good listener, on average we're not. Very early in my career I had a boss who would look at me with a pained expression as he attempted to restrain his mouth until the instant I finished a statement so he could start talking again. He was only listening for a break in the airwaves so he could again broadcast. Perhaps I needed to get to the point faster, but it was obvious from his subsequent statements that we had not, in fact, communicated. The distinction between listening merely to hear versus listening to understand is critical. Only the latter moves a conversation and relationship to a deeper level of connection. To the speaker, being heard and understood are reassuring, even compelling. Removing distractions and committing to listening to understand are intentional and wise choices. When I'm busy with a list of tasks and limited time, these actions can feel like a burden. But no list of to-dos is a greater investment or serves a higher purpose than pouring your life into another. Perhaps scheduling a time in which you can be completely present is a good response.

As I write, my eighth-grade son was ready to talk as I sat on the couch, across the room, working on my laptop. After a few minutes, I realized I wasn't going to finish work, and he wasn't going to be truly heard. Without a word, I shut the laptop and put it on the floor. Although he may not have realized it, he responded to that invitation to be understood, gathered a blanket, came across the room, and sat by me on the couch to tell me what he learned that day about building a computer. My small sacrifice to hear him gave us a father-son moment I hope neither of us will forget.

Being a member of an inner circle or personal truth-teller can take many forms. It's not formal. You may be the occasional friend in the golf cart, the routine life coach, or the random check-in phone call from an old friend. Regardless of form, making time to consider our role is a valuable exercise. Here are some questions to ask yourself.

- Do my words or presence have any impact?
- Can I be more intentional in the role I currently fill for this person?
- Have I been entrusted to study and consider their well-being and be an accurate mirror of truth for them?
- Am I orbiting them in the role of confident, encouraging friend, or bluntly corrective fighter pilot?

Ideally, I hope to be connected well enough and be wise enough to simply ask very good questions by which their own wisdom and creativity owns an insight or solution. Needing to be equally vulnerable as a supporting cell member, my responses might also refer to a more qualified expert or simply acknowledge, "I don't know, but I'll try to figure it out with you."

The morning following our team trespassing after the championship game, we cleaned up the now soggy toilet paper as students ringed the courtyard with smiles and cameras. The coach and school principal threatened to pull us from the state tournament. Newspaper and radio shows picked up the story. One witty reporter wrote, "Happy Hoopsters fare well on court. How will they fare in court?"

After a weekend of nosy church ladies questioning my salvation, I finally returned to school hoping for some normalcy. Some "friends" had defaced posters for the upcoming school musical. Flyers that had previously read "Fiddler on the Roof" were now colorfully edited with a big "R" to read "Riddler on the Roof." Winning the state championship a few weeks later seemed to heal the hurt feelings of our administrators and made a perfect conclusion to a wild end of the season.

As I remember the laughter of that night, it is obvious the roles of friends are central to the richness of our lives. We need to seek out those souls who embody the wisdom of Proverbs: "As iron sharpens iron, so one person sharpens another" (27:17 NIV). A discerning soul will grow to understand that perhaps the same person I boosted onto the roof in the middle of the night, who later sat by me in the police car, is probably not the one I should expect to sharpen my decision making. Equally important, perhaps the lives I touch need me to be the one to say, "Don't do anything stupid" instead of simply loaning them my glow-in-the-dark glasses.

THUNDERBOLT TAKEAWAYS

 ✘ Who do you listen to?
 ✘ Whom do you empower to tell you the truth?

Building or protecting an image is a near universal flaw that blocks our ability to be humble and to properly self-manage.

 ✘ What obstacles (such as lack of deep or quality connections, waiting for someone else to initiate, and fear of being vulnerable) are preventing you from having an inner circle of empowered truth-tellers?
 ✘ What new energy and initiative can you take to nurture and invite the potential for wisdom and connection through a truth-teller?
 ✘ When approached, how do you respond to feedback? Do you get defensive and quickly move to justify yourself? Are you able to navigate through your emotions or hurt to get to a point of growth and application, truly valuing the possible bruises from a friend?

✗ Who in your life right now needs your influence? How might you nurture the trust in your relationship to become a needed mouthpiece to express loving truth for someone else?

Let's tune-up those listening-to-understand skills:

✗ What might be hindering your ability to be present and listen well? Perhaps you're dealing with physical exhaustion, cultural barriers, illness, limited time, self-preoccupation, or an excessive need to "be heard." Whatever it is, identify it and own it.

✗ Be sure to ask open-ended questions (e.g., who, what, and how) that help you to grasp and clarify the other person's world and meaning.

Listen more deeply than simply the efficiency of facts, flaws in logic, or potential solutions. (Unfortunately, my default tends to be to shortcut listening, which can also stunt my growth.) What emotions and depth of stirring are the speaker experiencing? Why is their focus in the conversation so important to them?

✗ Restate the highlights of what the speaker has said, inviting their edits to hone your understanding, and then "wonder" together on what has been discussed to allow further reflection and exploration of meaning, purpose, and active listening. For example, "I wonder what some next steps might be?" or "I wonder what you're taking away from this experience?"

District champs cleaning up their mess after trespassing.

State champs two weeks later.
(Copyright © 1992 Lincoln Journal-Star; 1993 Lincoln Journal-Star)

14

MAN IN THE MIRROR

"What embitters the world is not excess of criticism,
but an absence of self-criticism."
—G. K. Chesterton

My younger brother is brilliant. An internal medicine and pediatric specialist, he was the valedictorian of his high school, a *summa cum laude* college graduate, a medical school top 10 percent honor society graduate, and following a four-year residency program, was asked to remain as chief resident. He's also taller than me. All of these facts make some stories more satisfying to tell.

He and his lovely new bride traveled to Banff National Park in Canada for their honeymoon. While lodging in a cabin small enough to simultaneously use the restroom, fry eggs, and watch TV, Eric and his wife headed out to go whitewater rafting. After his wife was given a wet suit, Eric was mistakenly handed the same size by the outfitter. After fighting his way into the wet suit and now unable to walk properly due to the tight fit, Eric huddled with the group-and-raft guide in what he terms a "Rated R" uniform for the day. As the tour guide gathered the group, he asked, "Who's been rafting before?"

Eric, perhaps emboldened with a degree of honeymoon machismo, raised his hand, indicating that he was, in fact, an experienced whitewater rafter. The tour guide looked at Eric and said, "You? Your helmet is on backwards."

Whether empathizing with Dr. Riddle or President Harrison, whether in a single moment or over the course of years, there are times when our perception of our skill set or role can take a rapid shift. President Harrison's perception error and most egregious mistake were not primarily the fault of his close friends or family but his own failure to come to terms with his condition, to embrace his own frailty, and to self-govern accordingly. Although his inner circle ought to have had the power and opportunity to tell him to put a coat on before the fateful inauguration, President Harrison's inability to identify and manage his insecurities blinded him to his need to wear a coat.

Business leaders teach that the ledger numbers are how your company speaks to you. Coaches have win-loss records and graduation rates to score their teams' performance and progress. Job performance metrics—like sales charts, patents awarded, the class test average of your students, or mergers negotiated—can provide clean numbers that paint a picture of how one is performing. Parents may look at the health, safety, and resiliency of their children while students can get a quick snapshot of their academic health from a GPA. Like President Harrison, I know that I'm too close to my own reflection to see things clearly. My self-perceptions can be vulnerable to oversights or blind spots. While relying on the wisdom of others and empowering their voice are keys to our health, we cannot outsource our responsibility for honest self-evaluation. We need to consider if we are able to conduct an honest self-evaluation and allow the data of our lives to inform that assessment. The tricky part of critical self-assessment is to find the narrow center road of truth and hope while avoiding a fall onto the side of the obtuse and oblivious or onto the side of those defeated members wallowing in self-loathing.

The fighter pilot debrief is a sacred and critical component of how America creates the best flying force in the world. Books, consultants, and best-selling authors detail elements of our debrief techniques for business and personal application. As young pilots, the presentation and adjustment to a highly focused critique of your entire performance can be shocking. Initially, I and other students often responded defensively, uncomfortable with the microscopic level of scrutiny and the demands of exceptional performance. However, the successful finishers are those able to separate personal value from personal performance and be driven more by improvement than paralyzed by hurt feelings. The graduate level of the debrief involves those who are mature enough to be able to critically and honestly self-assess, finding the most core lessons to be learned and then being able to instruct the performance of others from that perspective. Truthful, honest evaluation, not personally injurious critique, is the goal and is the hard work by which fighter pilots win.

Key to a successful debrief is determining the truth data. That is, what exactly was said on the radio, where precisely was your aircraft in space, and most telling, how does your HUD tape and digital data-link information validate or contradict your perceptions? HUD stands for Heads Up Display. HUD video is recorded from the vantage point of the cockpit. Every fighter sortie has a HUD tape as well as digital reconstruction capability. We need points of reference like this. At times we have an incredible amount of information to assess as we exert and exhaust ourselves physically flying a fighter jet and pulling G's. (Although the A-10 and close air support mission are generally kinder on the body than other missions and other airframes.) On top of that, we have to make decisions and orchestrate who lives and who dies on the battlefield. Sometimes pilots have so much going on that they struggle with what they call "helmet fires"—meaning, there was too much happening all at once, leading the pilot unable to mentally sort out all that occurred. In-flight sweat, task saturation, misprioritization, and hurled conflicting comments might be part of a mission reconstruction. But one debrief maxim surpasses them all: HUD tape don't lie. There must always be a place in our lives for truthful, unflinching, and objective data.

My jet climbed out past the gathering brown sandstorm near Ahmad al-Jaber Air Base in Kuwait in early 2003. I was flying as a wingman on another combat mission in the early stages of Operation Iraqi Freedom. Our planning that day had detailed potential target sets south of Baghdad, focusing on facilities of the Republican Guard at the Medina Division headquarters. We had completed our standard thorough mission planning, established some common reference points from the map study, looked at potential target imagery, and received an update on friendly troop locations and potential threat locations from our intelligence team and the army ground liaison officer.

Arriving over our target area, we matched up our eyeballs to what we had seen on the map, spoke with the ground controllers, and began dropping five hundred pound bombs on Medina Division HQ buildings. Sporadic antiaircraft fire became more concentrated on our area, exploding above and below us. I could see the distinctive four flashes of a firing S-60 a safe distance away.

Leaving smoldering ruins behind us and separating from the antiaircraft fire, we began to search the grid area of a reported artillery piece. Nearly twenty years ago, the A-10 was not yet the digitally interconnected airframe it is today, so my squadron did not have access to the game-changing targeting pod, and no A-10s had the cockpit multifunction displays to transmit those images with good picture quality. While working with my flight lead from a safe distance to locate the artillery piece, I alternated between peering through binoculars, moving my eyes across suspected reference points, and occasionally looking through my camera-enabled AGM-65 Maverick missile. I love the Maverick missile. There is a camera of sorts in the nose of the missile which, at the time, had a crude television monitor in the cockpit so you could "see" what the missile detected and then potentially lock-up a target and fire a missile that would self-guide all the way to impact. Locking up a target and then hammering down on the pickle button with your thumb, you would hold the button for what seemed like an eternity amid the temporal distortion commonly experienced by pilots, and the missile would launch off the rail like a freight train with ten thousand pounds of thrust. The TVM (television monitor) in the jet had poor fidelity even for that time. It had a green-tinted lens over the top and reminded me of the crude video pong screen of my childhood games. In fact, if I rolled in on a target with the sun over my shoulder, I would occasionally have to shield the glare with my right hand while flying with my left to try to see what was on the screen.

As we searched, there wasn't any human activity in the area, and obviously the artillery piece wasn't firing at the time or we would have been able to locate it. Our ground controller was persistent in the reported location and activity recently and wanted reassurance it would no longer be a factor as a threat to their team.

My flight lead passed an updated target location and rolled down the chute to take a Maverick shot. Unable to identify the target, he broke off his attack. I then took my turn down the chute, with my blood pumping full of "Buck Fever" and ready to shoot. I saw a surprisingly large and hot vertical tube on my TVM. I locked up the Maverick missile and launched half a house worth of taxpayer money toward the target. "Rifle!" I jubilantly declared as I pulled off target.

My flight lead and I waited for an impact and secondary explosions but didn't see any. He attempted another attack and again couldn't locate the artillery piece. Charged with my earlier success, I rolled down the shoot and again clearly saw the white hot vertical tube. "I've got it locked up. It's huge!"

"Rifle!" I called on the radio as another Maverick charged off the rail. Again, no obvious impact or secondary as it looked like it may have gone a little long, possibly overflying my desired impact point by a little bit. We continued searching for other artillery and encountered some other sporadic but not especially threatening antiaircraft fire. We hit Bingo fuel, meaning we were out of gas for the mission, so we headed back to base.

As I taxied the jet to park, my crew chief was fired up to see that his jet had dropped all the bombs and fired both missiles. "Empty wings" meant that his A-10 had taken the fight to the bad guys and his work had made it possible. The excited crew chief congratulated me. It is his jet after all; as the pilot, I'm merely entrusted with it for a time. We took a few pictures, and I gave him a Maverick "plug"[25] and a Mk-82 bomb lanyard hanging from the jet as souvenirs.

My flight lead and I finished our paperwork and excitedly headed to debrief to watch our HUD and TVM tape and evaluate our awesomeness. The 8mm tapes that recorded missions at the time were able to capture some sharper fidelity than we could see as pilots at speed and on the TVM. After critiquing my bomb passes, some good hits and desired effects on the targeted buildings, I cued up my first Maverick pass. And my stomach sank. I felt a little flushed and nauseous, a strange buzzing in my ears. Tape don't lie. I had fired two expensive Maverick missiles at what I thought was a white-hot artillery tube. I actually hit a warehouse doorway 40 yards downrange from our potential target area. I had locked the missiles on the sun-heated doorframe of a warehouse, which, too conveniently, looked just like an artillery tube to a fighter pilot who had his fangs out. The flight lead didn't need to say a thing; I deconstructed my errors for both of us. I refused any consolation that hoped the warehouse may have been a staging area for the enemy or some other speculative grasp.

Although not unkind, the debrief and tape review are candid, factual, and unflinching. Sometimes I might prefer to look away. But we don't look away and that's one reason why fighter pilots win. The cauldron of a debrief, including objectives intended, results measured, and lessons for improvement applied, provide the data, the heat, and the pressure necessary for refinement.

So how can we, without the advantage of a HUD tape and structured approach, invoke some measure of routine self-assessment that is not harsh or unkind but truly strives for objective data that might refine our character and elevate the quality of our impact on others while moving us along in a journey that moves us closer to being like Christ? An initial step is to acknowledge that, regardless of our confidence, comfort level, or the nice things people may say about us, there will always be room for growth and refinement in our lives. Tied to this knowledge is the fact that opening our eyes to see our faults, ranging from mildly annoying to darkly flawed, requires a courage that is more committed to growth than avoiding embarrassment or awkwardness. Not unlike the process to refine metal.

Refinement is a complex process of removing worthless impurities to get to the best version of a metal—or ourselves. I remember an engineer describing a historical method of smelting. Copper refinement requires an intense heat and chemical pairing to bring forward the pure and best elements of copper while also separating and exposing the residue and slag that had previously been completely embedded. Metal in a natural state is oxidized and impure. Likewise, the natural state of our character, without the disruptive process of confession, forgiveness, and refinement, is condemned to a base and deplorable condition. Introducing heat and pressure in our own lives has the potential to produce a similar purifying result. We have opportunity in hardship to demonstrate our best qualities and to rise to the occasion when it matters the most. Simultaneously, previously concealed weaknesses are moved to the forefront.

As both a combat commander and an earnest dad trying to make a disastrous military move go easier on my family, I've had the opportunity to see personal strengths and the slag of flaws in my own character be made separate and apparent. Before precise temperature measurement was possible, an ancient metal worker would draw the slag off the purifying metal and continue the refining until he saw a cue that his refinement was complete. That cue was the ability to now see his own reflection in the metal. In a similar way, the Lord can use difficulties that intensify the heat and pressure on us so as to refine us to the point that he might begin to see the reflection of his nature within us. We are his image-bearers, after all (Genesis 1:27). His desire is for us to partner with him in this process so we can better reflect his character and image instead of becoming obsessed with the injustice and discomfort of what we're experiencing. Likewise, the metal worker doesn't use fire because he hates the ore or because he wants to punish it. Rather, he uses the heat to remove the dross so that the purity of the metal is revealed.

Realizing our need to be refined and to commit to a personal debrief of sorts, despite the potential discomfort, leads us to searching out our own truth data. In the cockpit, we have panels full of instruments that provide immediate data that communicate the health and performance of our jet as well as if we are being potentially threatened. Attitude, altitude, and airspeed indicators, engine indicators, radar warning receiver, moving map displays, targeting pod video, and weapons systems all provide information perpetually. The term "cross-check" for pilots refers to the composite scanning across the array of instruments, gauges, and indicators to build our situational awareness and inform our decisions. Fixating on any indicator too long or routinely while excluding other informative gauges or instruments can prove fatal.

SEEDS is an acronym that can help us establish an internal cross-check of our lives to help us view data reflective of our own health and performance and to inform our decisions.[26] Some indications may be routinely positive while others might require our attention. Remember, ignoring an instrument in your cross-check could prove disastrous. Take a look at a few simple gauges that already exist in our lives and self-assess. These lifestyle considerations are able to increase our personal resilience in two ways: in a preventive manner decreasing risks of depression and anxiety, and in a restorative phase, helping us to recover from such hardships.

Social Support: Research findings continue to demonstrate that a key indicator of postoperative recovery, occasionally outdistancing even preexisting health, quality of surgeon, hospital, or income levels, was the social support network of the patient.[27] A social support network that is thriving has a positive presence of others in our lives that includes meaningful conversations and routine quality engagements with friends, neighbors, family members, and regular church or club participation. Positive social support is often typified by physical contact, verbal honesty (both affirming and challenging), and being emotionally invested and available. Negative data for our social support would be indicated by habitual conflict, distance, or difficulty connecting with others and loneliness.

Exercise: There is an exhaustive vault on the positive effects of routine exercise on physical as well as mental and emotional health. Exercise is the number one influence on biochemical activity capable of *greater* impact than both therapy and medical treatment. Exercise releases norepinephrine, a natural antidepressant. And the longer, more intense, more frequent the exercise, the greater the antidepressant effects: better memory, increased energy, self-mastery, greater likelihood of action versus emotional immobilization, and reducing the physically damaging effects of stress.

Education: Our interconnected nature of lifestyle, physiology, neurochemical status, and mental health corresponds to brain health. Feeding our brain often requires of us to do what we don't feel like doing. Moderate tension is good; it exercises neuroplasticity and the active sensors of our brain. Doing something new, becoming accustomed to being uncomfortable, and engaging in novel conversations or books are healthy activities to push us out of stagnation.

Diet: Food fuels our brain and provides the building blocks for our neurotransmitters. Our lifestyle and well-being are interconnected with what we eat and how stress effects our chemical makeup. For example, stress can deplete vitamins B, C, and potassium and increase cholesterol. Low vitamin B is associated with anxiety, depression, and difficulty concentrating, a negative mental bias, and sleep disruption. An over caffeinated diet, which is more than 250 milligrams a day, raises neurochemical indicators to what is considered a clinically stressful state. Consider that an eight ounce Starbucks can have 180 milligrams of caffeine and a can of Mountain Dew has 54 milligrams. A third cup of coffee for the day might contribute to not resting well.

Sleep: Hall of Fame football coach Vince Lombardi said, "Fatigue makes cowards of us all." Restorative sleep is critical to overall well-being. Recommendations to help set the stage for a good night's sleep include avoiding novelty at bedtime, planning the next day's activities even well before bedtime, and jotting down a to-do list at the last minute to get the items off your mind. Using white noise as a muffler, avoiding long naps, accomplishing exercise more than three hours before bedtime, keeping the room dark and cold, and not having a TV in the room all contribute to a better night's sleep.

Just as HUD tape doesn't lie, what kind of feedback does the data from your SEEDS cross-check say about your well-being? Just like in the aircraft, sometimes the amount of data might become overwhelming, and we become task saturated. As an easy method to move forward, I recommend tackling a few things rather than trying to handle everything at once. First, rather than consider an entire life-altering project, simply choose one area of your life that you would like to see refined. Then imagine that area of your life were a perfect ten out of ten. What would that look like? Define a perfect ten for you. What kind of activities, level of involvement, or health indicators would reflect that high scoring goal? And rather than attempt to leap from your current actual state to a perfect ten in multiple areas of your life, choose one thing to do that marches you in the direction of the ten. Leaning on the "SMART" goal's literature, be intentional in setting a goal that has these SMART qualities.

- Ensure your objective is *Specific* and *Measurable*—that is, you can clearly identify if you accomplished the goal or not.
- Additionally, make your goal *Achievable*. Dunking a basketball with a ten-foot-high hoop will never be an achievable goal for me.
- In the same way, goals should be *Realistic* and *Time* bound. Deadlines are sometimes the only stick to compel us forward. Set a plan in motion to accomplish your goal by a date marked on your calendar.

Understanding that our Creator loves us, that we may encounter fires of refinement throughout our lifetime, and that we are able to debrief our own experiences, successes, and failures all work together to help ensure that we learn the lessons most critical to us.

Now, as you make a few SMART goals, you will hit and miss a few, just like a fighter pilot on the bombing range. The most important part of the process is to learn why you got a hit and why you had a miss and be able to improve on the next effort. If you miss an objective, ask yourself why. Perhaps you need to find a more compelling goal, or you may require a more routinized practice level of accountability, or you may simply need to refine your plan and reattempt it. Over time, you will improve, you will get better.

In the days that followed my misses in Iraq, I was fortunate to fire several more Maverick missiles, including two on a single pass on a special operations mission. No more misses and, hollering delight, simultaneous explosions on two separate targets on one of the more satisfying missions of my life. Refinement isn't a comfortable process, but the wise will love the result.

THUNDERBOLT TAKEAWAYS

- ✔ Identify a single focus area needed for personal change, and, most importantly, consider why you've chosen that focus area. Your motivation and subsequent discipline to work toward change is directly connected to what drives you to pursue the outcome.
- ✔ Create a SMART goal to guide your efforts. When goals are too lofty or too difficult, it is hard to create any momentum and sustained effort. Small, achievable, sustainable, and behavior-altering goals will prompt your steps toward change.
- ✔ As you conduct your internal cross-check, I encourage you to challenge the natural human inclination to draw conclusions about ourselves and then only focus on the evidence that reinforces your beliefs. Whether in politics or personal well-being, each of us is vulnerable to dismissing evidence that doesn't fit our mental model. When it comes to your health, challenge the thoughts that physically, emotionally, or mentally are in a fixed state. They may hinder your ability to recreate yourself in some way.
- ✔ Approach change as a collaborative effort between yourself and the Lord, as well as between you, a close family member, or a friend. Perhaps start with the short prayer: "Lord, thank you for your grace and how patient you are in making me more like you. Guide my thoughts and mind to where I need to change so I might be more healthy for myself and others and for service in your kingdom."

An air force display of mutual support. Our flying tactics have a built-in social support network with paired wingmen on every sortie. This four-ship was my A-10 final flight as the 303rd fighter squadron commander. (Tommy Davis / Instagram @tommyd_photography)

15

REDLINE LIVING

"Any fool can make things bigger, more complex, and
more violent. It takes a touch of genius—and a lot
of courage—to move in the opposite direction."
—Albert Einstein

"Come to me, all you who are weary and burdened, and I will give
you rest. Take my yoke upon you and learn from me, for I am
gentle and humble in heart, and you will find rest for your souls.
For my yoke is easy and my burden is light."
—Jesus (Matthew 11:28-30 NIV)

Ludicrous speed.
Light speed.
Supersonic.
Frantic.
Too busy.

Those seem to be the words most friends and coworkers use to describe the busyness of work, parenting, youth activities, and recreation to the degree that can win bragging rights. There exists a cultural allure to living at maximum capacity. We even have access to YouTube videos of those individuals pushing human limits to and beyond their max. Be it BASE jumping, those amazing flying squirrel suits that daredevils wear and leap from clifftops, or fortune seekers converting monstrous financial risks into riches, there is an appeal to brinksmanship and living on the sharpened edge between glory and disaster. We are captivated by watching a scene where there is no margin for error, seemingly no cushion or safety net for anything short of perfection. The adventures move toward near superhuman and mythical performance levels . . . or utter ruin.

Everything has a limit of design. Chipsets have limits to their computational operations per second and latency, aircraft have airspeed and G-tolerance limits, a budget has fiscal limits, and even our greatest warriors on earth have physical, mental, and emotional limits, regardless of how impressive their capacity to suffer and strive. The reality of limitations is a truth with universal applications. Design specifications of aircraft engine performance or how many hours a truck driver may be on the road are calculated to keep equipment and people a safe distance from disaster. Safety margin is a design consideration.

In my A-10, as in all airframes, there are volumes of numbers to memorize across dozens of gauges and systems that indicate the performance parameters of each component of the aircraft: a proper zone of temperatures for exhaust gas temperature, interstage turbine temperature, auxillary power unit start-up temperatures, oil pressure limits, and G limits based on fuel loads. And the list goes on for days. While those numbers are likely stored somewhere in my memory, the quick in-cockpit cheater check is to look at the little gauge arm and see if it is pointing at a green piece of tape or red piece of tape: green, good; red, bad.

An odd and dangerous characteristic is that the jet is capable of operating and feeling normal even when the engine gauges are pointing at the red line and operating beyond design limits. There is even a switch on the fuel control panel labeled "OVERRIDE" that will disconnect protective fuel limiting to allow for about 15 percent more thrust in power critical situations. These are emergencies. For instance, losing an engine on takeoff when the aircraft is at its heaviest and slow, you may need emergency power to safely maintain flight.

It seems that life places us in seasons in which we live in the redline, exceeding our personal limits. Some of us take up seemingly permanent residence there. Exceeding these design limits may feel normal at times, but the reality is that damage will soon come. It is inevitable. That's why redline living is dangerous. Moving our capacity switch to OVERRIDE may have become our new normal, but it shouldn't be. We are flirting with disaster.

Our A-10 initial training occurs at Davis-Monthan Air Force Base in Tucson, Arizona. An incredible place to fly jets, Tucson itself sits in a small bowl of mountains with incredible tactical training ranges and great weather with blue skies so clear you can see over 30 miles most days. And there is plenty of room to skim along low to the ground. Part of our training syllabus includes night flying. When it's dark out, it's harder to see. With limited night-flying hours prior to Tucson, I had to learn to trust the laws of aerodynamics to work in the dark and find some way to interpret which small lights were my instructor's jet and which light was actually Jupiter. On one occasion, an instructor—an old guy no one trusted—told me to rejoin on him from a few miles away. He then turned his position lights to steady and then off and made a turn. I then flew 10 miles, mistakenly, toward Jupiter. That desert sky is really clear! That was an embarrassing student moment. I also didn't remember any exciting fighter pilot movie scenes or thrilling air shows at night. My thinking at the time was that this night flying was simply a necessary evil.

After a few night missions, we began flying with night-vision goggles. Although an adjustment to fly with what feels like small binoculars stuck in front of your face, the goggles are amazing at magnifying preexisting light beyond the spectrum of the human eye and giving you some amazing capability. On an early NVG (night-vision goggle) training sortie, climbing out of the bowl of mountains near Tuscon, I had just flipped my goggles down when I heard a loud pop and the right wing of the jet drop off a little bit. As I looked under the goggles, a number two engine temperature gauge was climbing rapidly through 900 degrees as the RPM was winding down. Quickly the red fire light drew my disbelieving gaze. Gratefully, the A-10 has two motors, and although lacking the confidence experience brings, I shut down the engine that stalled and worked my way through our checklist with a patient instructor. As I turned toward the final approach, I rehearsed my emergency egress training—what I needed to do to get out and away from the jet quickly. Our class coincidentally had a refresher a few days previously, and I remembered the instructor saying you could just swing out of the cockpit, hang from the canopy rail, and drop to the ground. A friend chided me, saying he didn't recommend that for me as the canopy was still three times as high as I was tall. We all laughed, but something must have stuck in my subconscious about proving him wrong.

Fortunately, the final approach and landing was uneventful, with some minor asymmetric, crooked flying due to having only one working motor. As I rolled down the runway, firetrucks with lights spinning pulled onto the runway and chased me as I rolled to a stop. I popped the canopy open, disconnected from the ejection seat, and swung my legs over the side of the jet. I held on to the canopy rail for a second and then let go. And then fell what felt like five stories. My feet had swung under me a little bit when I slammed onto the ground bouncing from my heels directly to the back of my skull. As I opened my eyes, lying flat on the runway, I was seeing stars. It took me a moment to determine if they were from my awkward fall or the night sky. Like a slow-motion video, the fire chief in a silver foil suit leaned forward into my view, looked down at me, and said, "Are you okay, son? That didn't look too good."

As happens with most embarrassing moments in a fighter community, we require exhaustive and entertaining retellings of such buffoonery to an audience of your brothers and sisters of the fighter squadron. One key event of sacred debauchery in which these stories are embellished and retold is a naming ceremony. Earning a fighter pilot call sign is a complex mix of kangaroo court, cherished storytelling that requires adherence to at least 10 percent truth, and most importantly, a recognition that you are now considered a worthy warrior by your peers. New to this culture, I found myself standing at the front of a packed squadron bar, being directed to retell my engine fire story as my potential call signs are being carefully considered by what looks to me to be little more than an angry mob. Between cheers and jeers, I got to the part where I fell to the ground. My storytelling skills were on training wheels. Additionally, I grew up in a conservative Christian home, and we didn't use profanity or vulgarity with words like *fart* or *butt*. So I told the inebriated audience, who was considering my future call sign as a fighter pilot, that I had fallen right on my "fanny." It was a word my dad and old women with knitting needles used in place of *butt*.

My fraternity of warriors erupted in mocking laughter as one guy in the back hollered out, "I nominate Fanny!" Then the chanting began: "Fanny! Fanny! Fanny!" I was nauseated, imagining my career call sign as a fighter pilot was going to be "Fanny," complete with nametag. I didn't remember any History Channel fighter pilot documentaries with anyone named Fanny. Was I going to have to sign a career of air force memos as Fanny?

Gratefully, a wise, gray-haired colonel from the back announced, "No, Fanny doesn't pass the Nellis test!" I had no idea what the Nellis test was, but I was in violent agreement that, most assuredly, Fanny didn't pass the test, so the disappointed mob tagged me something else.

While humble beginnings and rites of passage are common to achieving goals and traversing the difficult journeys of life, no one wants to be reduced to identifying who they are solely by what they produce. I have yet to ever hear of a deathbed confession in which someone wishes they had stayed late at the office one more time, had squeezed in one more sales trip, or taken more phone calls from work while on vacation. In a culture that moves to increasing digital connections that create a vacuum of loneliness and shallow personal connections, relationships haven't the fertile time or personal margin to bear fruit. An enlightened approach, however, realizes how important it is that we spend our time on what we most value so we don't end up with a heart full of regret when life has passed us by.

My ill-conceived leap from the cockpit was born from a lack of awareness of my physical limits as well as decisions tainted with vain pride. The glowing red fire light within a cockpit is a blessing really. It is the most obvious signal of something terribly wrong demanding that priorities must be changed immediately to avert disaster. Unfortunately, no glowing fire light so clearly demands immediate action when potential disaster approaches us through our finances, our relationships, our career ambitions, or our health. If we are diligent in investigating, if we are trailing smoke from our personal number one engine across any areas of our lives, we must build time to identify and cross-check indicators of our own wellness. There are consequences for us and those connected to us if we slam the throttles forward, ignore the fire lights, or jump out of the cockpit in an unnecessary hurry.

One of my favorite aspects of flying fighter jets is that the demands of combat missions—complex missions that have a lot of assets integrating firepower—is that you are engrossed, focused and fully present. No distractions about to-do lists, emails, kids' practices, or ruminations about "what did they mean when they said so and so" have room to creep to the front of your mind. As Winston Churchill said, "You are never so alive as following a near miss." While difficult to match a combat-peaked sense of being present, I know it's achievable even in everyday life. I admire, for example, my wife's ability to begin each day quieted before the Lord. The prayers, reading, and reflection each morning are a model of grappling with what is deeply important and worthy of her best energy versus what is temporary, worrisome, and relegated to being accomplished and finished but not taking up residence in her heart.

In contrast, I tend to hustle out the door, imagining Christ awkwardly hurrying along behind as I tell him to get in the car. He takes a quick step and loses a sandal, then gets his robe caught hanging out the door closing it too quickly to avoid me backing over him. I race out to attack the next set of tasks, hoping the Lord, who wants to give me rest and wisdom, will carry my burden amid a world of flailing demands. I want him to keep up with me and bless me as I race past.

It is difficult in our American culture to divorce our identity from our productivity. I think a great Christian witness is to honor the Lord with excellence in all the types of work and family-rearing that we're fortunate to do. Both the challenges we encounter and the work we accomplish carry a deeper purpose to foment and reveal rich character rather than simply being necessary or treated as trivial tasks that solely exist to get checked off of a to-do list.

Scanning the gauges in your own cockpit, looking at several areas of your life, look to see if your readings are in the green zone (healthy), the yellow zone (at risk), or the red zone (demanding immediate action). Glancing at your use of money, time schedules, health of your relationships, parenting, and career management is a good place to follow up our previous chapter's work on well-being. Hardship or challenge in these areas of life are common to all of us. Less common is the courage to patiently self-assess and move our lives back toward living in the green zone—a zone with margin for rest and recuperation that may build a reservoir of strength for those times when we need to surge ahead and select override in an emergency.

Finances are perhaps the clearest opportunity to see if we are making decisions that allow for margin. Financial stress is routinely cited as a leading cause of divorce with 86 percent of couples who have married in the last five years starting out in debt. Additionally, nearly 34 percent of those aged eighteen to twenty-nine feel hopeless or despair regarding their financial future.[28] Calendars routinely fill to overflowing as Americans average longer work days than in the 1950s and take only slightly more than two weeks of vacation a year. The workplace can be a place of stress, driving us to our limits as 70 percent of workers said they feel stress on the job and another 25 percent said that yelling and verbal abuse were common due to workplace stress.[29]

The weariness of life encroaches on the home as parents and children average about 40 minutes of interaction a day with no distinctions made for the type or quality of interaction. Some occasions, like on the weekends, might reflect more time per day that parents spend with their children, but these hours are often marked by fatigue and watching TV rather than making deep family connections.[30]

A University of London study concluded that living at the red line— namely, failing to manage our reactions to chronic, unrelenting stress—were more dangerous risk factors for cancer and heart disease than either smoking or eating high cholesterol foods.[31]

Since all of us are human and have a range of green to redline responses, I encourage you to speak to those closest to you about their perception of your proximity and life near redline. Even though I may struggle to interpret what I see on a single gauge, a wingman who hollers into the radio, "Lead, you're on fire!" removes all doubt. Empower those closest to you to speak truth into your life and provide a perspective that you may lack. My dad, brother, and a friend from my time in Texas are the ones most capable of looking at the activities of my life and discerning if I'm trailing smoke or humming along for a short but necessary season in override. Persistent fatigue or distraction, chronic poor sleep, and having little pleasure or energy for what you've previously enjoyed are all signs of trailing smoke.

A part of walking back to the green zone is to learn what is most restful and beneficial to your overall wellness. As time off or vacation opportunities approach, I quickly pack recreation, entertainment, family outings, or exercise into that precious window of time. While recreation provides sweetness to life, it is difficult to savor and thrive in any situation when exhausted. Rest is God's design for us to gain strength, heal, and recover (Mark 2:27–3:5). When tired, our personal stress thresholds are lowered, and events that may normally be green-zone conditions or yellow-zone risks can rapidly accelerate to redline crises simply because of our emotional depletion, reduced optimism, or impaired judgment. When no longer functioning in the manner we were designed, when weary, we become increasingly vulnerable to careless people decisions and moral compromises, and consumed with instant results. To step away from redline living is to begin to find a place for quality rest.

The human capacity to perform and produce under the most amazing of circumstances is astounding. Incredible stories of heroic bravery and survival through the most horrific circumstances are universally inspiring as we see persons push beyond what we were convinced were human limits of perseverance, sacrifice, or love. Each of those stories reflect a temporary and epic season of life requiring them to live in redline, to have activated personal

OVERRIDE switches for survival. Warnings from the A-10 technical order make clear that OVERRIDE only exists for emergency situations. OVERRIDE is not designed to amplify daily output capacity that drains us of all energy and time for the important, soulful, and spiritual parts of life. Caution statements for OVERRIDE also warn that operating engines above normal temperature range should be for the absolute minimum time necessary to get to a safe condition, for damage will occur, and the flight characteristics will be different than how the jet normally flies. It should not be routine for the A-10 or ourselves to operate in emergency mode. If I was in the habit of exceeding engine temperatures on my A-10 every time I flew, you can imagine that the crew chief and my leadership would not tolerate the damage I was causing. Why then should my coworkers, family, or friends tolerate me being changed, damaged, and unavailable as a daily occurrence?

To operate at our best, within the green zone of God's design limits, we must push back against the culture that confuses being rested with being apathetic and misplaces our validation and identity in terms of productivity. Working with teams across the US Department of Defense, nonprofits, the tech sector, and in academia, a common curse is to confuse being busy with being effective. Busyness, then, becomes misconstrued as having value. On the other hand, searching out and honoring my own limits and conserving selections of OVERRIDE for only those epic situations demanding emergency actions will allow me to be more present and at my best for others on a daily basis while avoiding redline living.

THUNDERBOLT TAKEAWAYS

- ✗ You are more than you produce.
- ✗ Productivity is not the same as life meaning. You are more than what you do.
- ✗ Selecting OVERRIDE may be necessary for a season of your life, but it should not be idealized and reinforced as a preferred lifestyle.
- ✗ What seasons of OVERRIDE have you experienced, and what were the effects?

✗ Are these seasons unique or common? Have you begun to experience symptoms of burnout from these seasons, such as sleep disruption, absence of a sabbath or time off, preoccupation with work or a problem that routinely distracts you from being fully present at home or with others, loss of joy in life, or a severe drop in energy to do even what you enjoy?

✗ As we've practiced our cross-check before, take a look at each of these areas of your life and ask, "Am I in the green, yellow, or red zones for health and intentionality?"

- Schedule: How effective is your time management when it comes to work, tasks outside of career, time with family, and regular rest? Do you spend time and energy distracted or concerned about things over which you have no control or influence? How might you direct your energy and focus back to those areas in your life where you do have some specific control or influence? Finally, to be grounded spiritually amid a world of hurry, are you prioritizing any time for reading Scripture, reflecting, praying, and contemplating how you will respond to what you've learned?

- Money: Do you have significant stress about money? Are you intentional with your spending, saving, and giving, and disciplined in a budget? How often are you distracted or fearful about money and why?

- Relationships: Have you grown cold or distant from others you love? Do you struggle with loneliness? Do you have any significant relational conflicts that you need to resolve? Are you able to identify your need for deep and quality connections, and do you know how to go about nurturing those?

- Career: Are the demands and fulfillment of your career manageable? Do you have a sense of purpose that can carry you through the inevitable droughts of life regardless of your occupation?

✗ Are these or any other areas of your life so stressed that a "wingman" in your life would say, "Hey! You're trailing smoke!"? *You* might think you're juggling life well, but what do those closest to you think?

✗ What are some steps, some gradual or others dramatic, that would move you toward a safe green zone?

16

NOT EVERYONE MAKES THE TEAM

"OK, let's see what kind of hand I've been dealt."
—Coach Norman Dale, *Hoosiers*

"Do nothing from selfish ambition or empty conceit, but in humility regard others as better than yourselves. Let each of you look not to your own interests but to the interests of others."
—Paul (Philippians 2:3-4)

y college transcript reads like a patchwork quilt loosely stitching classes from a number of unrelated schools and courses, including motorcycle repair at a local community college to working as a research assistant in behavioral modification at the University of Nebraska Medical Center. Reflecting a bit of wanderlust and a range of interests, I surprisingly spent three great years in the same place and received my bachelor's degree from Evangel University. Evangel is a small Christian liberal arts school in southern Missouri. I was blessed to meet my wife there and connected with a group of great friends.

Although plausibly on campus to earn a degree, my friends from Krause First North (K1N) and I spent most waking hours practicing, planning, cherishing, and trash talking every moment of a rivalry-riddled intramural sports program. We also prioritized time to scavenge for free food and serve on a predictable rotation of delivering one another to the emergency room following the endless line of pranks or impressive feats of strength that had almost succeeded. At one point I had lobbied the Cox Medical Center for gold member parking for K1N outside of the ER.

I loved the group of guys on our dormitory floor. The dorm hall itself stunk like dirty laundry and ketchup and was generally damp. A mysterious drip fell from the ceiling in the middle of the hall leaving a large ring of perpetually wet carpet on the floor. We ruled that if you were ever struck by the drip, you had just received a mystical anointing of higher purpose and were responsible for that week's devotions, which were invariably cancelled due to a conflict with the intramural schedule.

We had a great mix of student athletes. A former point guard from the University of New England was my roommate. My best friend was an all-state football player from Nebraska. A wrestler across the hall had placed third in the New York high school state tournament, and he had played receiver for the Evangel football team. A former lineman and a former linebacker for Evangel, a high school pitcher and hockey player, a soccer player and a handful of other athletic bodies made for a great group of competitive friends who loved sports, loved the Lord, and learned to love each other.

We obviously had several guys on the floor who were at Evangel, strangely, for reasons other than intramurals but who were part of the K1N family and would join the loud gaggle of bodies each night heading to the cafeteria for dinner.

And then there was Ken.

Ken was not an athlete. He was built short and wide and had the kind soft smile of a friend. Ken was quickly adopted into the K1N family. After a few months of cheering us on at games and being indoctrinated of sorts, he marveled at how strange it was for him to catch an orange from someone at dinner. Dressed comfortably in worn-out denim, he became our floor mascot of sorts and allowed us to rub his head for good luck.

Arriving at our last night of the school year, enjoying the best of friends that had gathered on K1N from Maine to California, someone (no one is sure who) determined that we needed to engage in some mild mischief aimed squarely at a sister college across town. Affiliated with the same church denomination, Central Bible College (CBC) was a pastoral and ministry training college while Evangel was the liberal arts school. You can imagine the rivalry that virtually insisted we harass CBC in some way. A quick multipronged assault was planned where Team Alpha was to drop some smoke bombs in Flowers Hall (the same female-only dorm my mom had lived in twenty years before) while, with precise military synchronization, Team Bravo was to launch a mortar type assault of eggs on CBC's year-end gathering around the bonfire. I and the wrestler were deemed slippery enough for the brazen Team Alpha breach of Flowers Hall, while Bravo planned to safely launch their ordnance from a considerable distance in the woods. Like medieval archers attempting to engage from a distance, Ken fell in with Team Bravo. Outfitted in all black, we parked our assault vehicles: a four-door Dodge and a small Plymouth hatchback. We left the cars a few blocks away and straight up the street from the target area

Mission execution seemed flawless to Team Alpha. We silently sprinted through the dorm, dropping a few hissing smoke bombs as I swept past someone who never even turned their back to look. Cackling with laughter, we exploded out the back door, lept over an amorous couple snuggling on the stairs, and tumbled down a small slope. We went across a creek and headed back to our exfiltration coordinates—that is, parking spot. Team Bravo slowly and loudly made their way back to the cars.

As we settled in the vehicles, we saw the flashing lights of the campus security heading toward us. We scrambled from the cars and headed for the woods on foot. A few hours later, I found my way back to my dorm room where my father, a pastor and proud CBC alumnus, was waiting for me as he was helping get me home the next day. A gaggle of team members barged into the dorm room still dressed in black. They were muddy and sweaty and indebted to somebody's ex-girlfriend who drove out to pick us up from a remote gas station. Everyone presumed that the presence of my ordained pastor dad could thwart any unwelcome inquiries from the authorities.

I got up the next morning, took my last final exam, and loaded the car to return home.

A few weeks later, I received a phone call from the Krause Hall Residence Director who had been informed of my involvement in the CBC raid. Apparently, our mascot, our own amicable but unathletic Ken, had been unable to evade the security team and was found with two eggs, now broken, oozing down the front of his denim. Faced with the harsh reality of Christian school interrogation, Ken squealed and turned state's evidence, giving up my name and a few others. We couldn't believe it. Of Ken we thought, *Broken eggs in your pockets? Are you kidding? You can't even underhand roll them away from yourself?*

This wasn't all, though. We also found out that the attendants at the bonfire we had interrupted were engaged in a prayer vigil. Perhaps predictive of my future as a fighter pilot and short stint as a youth pastor, I couldn't imagine a better time to attack than when everyone's eyes were closed.

I paid my portion for the damages and was placed on shameful "social probation," which I'm still not sure exactly what that meant. I was also stripped of my assignment the following year which was supposed to be representing Evangel by hosting visiting students. It was probably better for me to have been fired before the school year started as, most likely, hosting visiting students would have been a conflict with the sacred intramural schedule.

Despite my nomadic college experience, nothing can bond you closer together with a group this side of combat than eating, sleeping, suffering, laughing, and getting in trouble together. That sense of team and family brings a fraternal language and commitment that are unique and special. That sense of belonging and having a role amid a band of brothers (or sisters) are part of what drew me to flying jets and being a part of a fighter squadron. As we stood in one another's weddings and moved to our respective corners of the country, sending birth announcements over the years, we inevitably drifted apart. Still, these are the kind of relationships that allow a phone call and quick connection that manages to transcend miles and years.

I've never seen or spoken to Ken after our CBC raid. Rejoining after the summer, we joked that KIN had placed a price on his head for going against the family. Everyone knows you never go against the family, and perhaps that's what spooked him out of returning. I don't know why he didn't come back. I've always assumed it was for reasons unrelated to the raid and more likely due to finances or a change of career choice. I was a floor president and intramural captain—ringleader is a better title. I didn't realize it then, but taking care of Ken, or my failure to take care of him, was a small-scale lesson of what being a follower of Christ and a leader, regardless of magnitude, asks of us.

Although a loyal mascot, at least until under duress, Ken was a hanger-on who never found a critical role on the team, and at no point did I consider how he might better fit within our group. He couldn't run or throw, so escape driver was likely a better role for him, and perhaps we could have gotten away clean had we placed him in a job that he could have done well.

Companies spend millions on trying to find the right people and then additional millions to try to get them properly trained and placed within the company. The reality is, not everyone fits, and very few fit perfectly. The 98 percent of average people like myself must attempt to modify our efforts, focus, interests, behavior, or even personality to fit into the job, family, or social situations in which we find ourselves. We are not adapting to become something else but to simply ease or improve our impact or ability to function. And depending on the degree of modification, the effort required may vary from minimal inconvenience to paying a significant personal cost in energy or emotion to adjust or succeed in an environment we find difficult.

Long before one goes against the family, I've always approached personnel, teams, or groups with the question, "How do I win with the hand I've got?" In other words, how do we minimize our weaknesses and align our strengths and talent to be the best team or most lethal force possible? Certainly, when on offense, whether in combat or with a team or even in business, we're looking to exploit an opponent's weakness at precisely the right time with the maximum impact. This is a classic personnel and tactical challenge that requires a deft touch for each member to fill their role, and perhaps not the role they've dreamt for themselves, with an energy and effectiveness that charges all members. It is a leadership puzzle to blend the structural and human resource frames of organizational alignment with finding members the proverbial right seat on the bus. Whether conveyed in my office as a fighter squadron commander, in a sweaty huddle of teammates, or over coffee in a corporate office, leaders need to respond in a couple of key ways to the Ken in their midst who may be leaking egg down the denim jeans of your team.

One important response is to avoid confusing what may be Ken's current lesser value to the team with lesser value as a person. If we approach Ken with marked empathy, then his current poor fit should not result in us being dismissive of all subsequent roles for Ken or helping find a more fulfilling future for Ken in a different situation. I refuse to forget that, as a leader, I need to optimize performance, but that doesn't mean I skip my responsibility as a caretaker to those under my watch.

The apostle Paul would remain countercultural to some of the hypercompetitive industries of today. I try to invite his words to change my heart and mature my decisions in the myriad of roles we all inevitably fill. "Do nothing from selfish ambition or empty conceit, but in humility regard others as better than yourselves. Let each of you look not to your own interests but to the interests of others" (Philippians 2:3–4). Paul challenges us, looking over the still wet ink of his letter to Philippi and into our eyes. Paul was tenacious in life and ministry. And yet, he strived not to let others fall through the cracks, thinking they didn't matter or that no good fit could be found for them. Likewise, I am not allowed to look over my shoulder and say that the interests of other people are the job of my church or my government and not mine. As I consider my heart, Paul isn't convinced by arguments that my company is socially responsible and makes the world a better place and then, by extension, so do I. Although noble and wonderfully socially responsible, the generosity of my favorite sneaker company or coffeeshop is a critical heartbeat removed from the tenderness and responsiveness of my own soul that Paul is after. To satisfy his charge to be personally vested in the well-being of others, we need to be aware of the dangers of "click-activism" where we do "good" simply by doing our deeds online or by passive involvement in which my purchase of new stuff enables a distant good deed. That inoculates us from tangible service, insulates us from being deeply moved and changed by another's condition, and attempts to excuse us from the intimate level of personal accountability faith and life demand.

To regard others as better than ourselves turns all stratified systems of education or pedigree or wealth on their head. Paul makes clear that each of us, including those of us who are leaders, exemplify understanding that *our* time, the money in *our* pocket, and the energy *we* wake up with are to be available to serve the interests of others. When I apply this to my own life, I now realize that I need to be willing to release my best Team Alpha members to do something else if it is in their best interests. Even more, I need to help facilitate that dream or next step for them. And I need to invest of myself to help shape or transition those Kens out there still looking for a place. We ought to be able to look at each Ken and think, *I may need to dig a little, and I might prefer to do something else with my time, but where can I place, refer, or train Ken to be at his personal best?* Ken deserves the chance to work hard and be at his best, not because of altruism, but because as a fellow child of the King, you and I may be the one drop of water or sun that moves him toward blooming fully into the calling and role for a greater good for himself and for infinite purpose.

A second and equally critical role for Ken's journey is to provide a direct, tactful, and truthful reflection of his current fit or lack of it. This is the more difficult action of the two discussed here for leaders. This is a responsibility that good leaders embrace with both courage and grace. I say *courage* because plenty of leaders avoid delivering difficult news at all costs, and either deliver no news, which is worse, or ask others to take care of the mess. I say *grace* because Ken's ears need to hear a difficult truth from a voice that sounds more like an empathic partner rather than a foul critic. Ken's heart and energy need to be lifted and redirected, not ignored or trampled. While a great deal of literature discusses getting people on the right seat of the bus and optimizing roles of members, the heart of this direct conversation begins with, "Ken, this doesn't seem like it's working to me; is this working for you?" And this is when discernment is critical. For a select few, there is no seat on anybody's bus they could productively belong. Considering others better than ourselves does not mean we are burdened to make room for toxic or dysfunctional fools and those who come alive at creating dissension. As Christ walked away from such people in the Scriptures or allowed them to walk away from him,[32] we, too, are free to throw those virally toxic souls off or under the bus. Presuming that your Ken is bringing effort, initiative, and a good attitude, he deserves our best effort for either a seat or a transition.

As an accountable leader, I can't dilute a performance standard or marginalize overall effectiveness for an extended period to simply be charitable. The challenge placed before Ken is if he can embrace and excel in a new role, or if a loss of status or responsibility becomes fatal to the existing arrangement. Ken might also feel a great sense of relief that someone is willing to partner in finding him a better bus seat or even a new bus. There have certainly been seasons of time when I was Ken and others made room for me, invested the additional time in training me, or finding a seat for me. As courage and grace have been extended to me in so many areas of my life, I am called to do the same.

THUNDERBOLT TAKEAWAYS

- ✗ Warning: Do not confuse another's worth as a person with their giftedness (or lack thereof) in a given system (e.g., college sports, work staff, or church member).
- ✗ Are you leading all of your team or office or family well, or are some people getting lost in the shuffle? Who are they? Why do you think they are getting lost?
- ✗ How are you focused on finding a way to win with those people and resources you have? Or do you feel like you are losing energy, becoming disillusioned or frustrated that the people around you "aren't good enough"?

- Is there a Ken in your team who has the heart to contribute but requires some effort or training to locate the best possible fit for him or her? How do plan to help this person transition?

- Is an intellectually honest and unbiased gathering of assessment data or facts sacred to you or your team when assessing performance, productivity, and personnel?

- How are you refining your ability to deliver difficult, truthful news with courage and grace? Can you lead these conversations with respect, honesty, and quality dialogue about potential next steps?

- Are you able to assume a humble posture to receive the same treatment and words from honest and necessary feedback? To hear both good and bad news and to define any next steps forward?

- Name someone in your circle of influence who would benefit from the sun or water you might uniquely deliver to their faith or career or to finding a place or tribe that provides a much better fit.

- How and when do you plan to deliver that sun or water?

- Where are you personally serving or sacrificing for others? Are you willing to serve in a way that may move or even change your own heart? Or have you, perhaps unknowingly, become safely insulated from the difficult needs of others by using "click-activism" or some other approach that keeps you personally uninvolved?

17
SEASON'S HIGHLIGHT

"Upon the fields of friendly strife are sown the seeds that
on other days, on other fields, will bear the fruits of victory."
—General Douglas MacArthur

"Freely you have received; freely give."
—Jesus (Matthew 10:8 NIV)

"Good will come to those who are generous and lend freely,
who conduct their affairs with justice."
—Psalm 112:5 NIV

I stood at the 13-yard line looking at the opponent's defense. Nearly every player in their blue shirts was stacked up on the line of scrimmage, facing the ball on his own 3-yard line. Our team faced them in our cardinal jerseys. It was a cold, gray day in Missouri with a light drizzle starting as we played in our opponent's hometown. I smirked, which I'm told I do too often, and shook my head in disbelief. Then I felt my throat catch and my eyes get moist. I looked at the ground and blinked. I smiled wider and thought we couldn't cue up a better season-ending opportunity for this little group of young boys. Predictably, I learned a lot from trying to love and lead this group of players and parents.

Our lives interconnect with the lives and patterns of others. This connection is more than just an awareness of those around us; it's also a deep linkage that operates in mutually beneficial ways or harmful dysfunction. Decisions and efforts I make, with either positive or negative effect by connection and extension, transmit benefit or harm throughout the entire group. Whether formal or informal, groups can be any set of relationships in which we orbit: work, family, social clubs, neighborhoods, parents, and so on. Systems theory tells us we don't function in isolation; rather, we operate in complex relationships that integrate with the behaviors and dynamics of others. This is a radically different view than what a Sicilian secretary from my fighter squadron said. She told me that each pilot "Seems to walk around as a zipper-suited sun god about whom the world orbits." Whether Psychology 101 or free verse Sicilian musings, kids can teach us a lot about how we ought to behave and where we actually fit in the grand universe.

I have always loved football. I thought of going pro, but I was no good and small. I made up for this by being slow. Surprisingly, it didn't work out. Growing up in Nebraska means you have a genetic and cultural predisposition that loves football and has an innate understanding of the importance of corn and beef, even if raised as a small city kid like myself. Obediently, I loved football and played in the house, knocking over lamps. I also tore holes in the knees of my pants in the vacant lot across the street. As a means of passing this important legacy to my son, I coached his youth football teams for six or seven years.

Our first year, I enjoyed working with a group of nineteen first graders. God bless our teachers! Our games looked less like football than the running of the bulls in Pamplona, with little players scampering wildly in all directions, confused if they were on offense or defense and if they were supposed to be running onto the field or heading to the sidelines. The league insisted on playing eleven on eleven on a 100-yard field. We had a seven-year-old player score on a 90-yard touchdown run at the end of our first game. He plunged into the line with both hands over the ball, got lost in the scrum, and rumbled outside for the next 85 yards, hunched over the ball all the way to the opposite end zone. The elapsed time on the play was about sixty-nine seconds. I'm pretty sure he stopped for a water break and orange slice mid play.

We switched the next year to a seven-on-seven league better suited for sharing the ball and playing fast. My son, Jake, played center and linebacker and bounced around to whatever spot I needed. We also had a couple of gifted little athletes, Cole and Logan, both able to throw and catch and make people miss while also being smart and anticipating plays on defense. I also met a new player that year. He was a second grader who already nearly looked me in the eye, smiled sweetly, and weighed the same I had weighed when I was sixteen. His impressive frame was paired with an equally impressive name, Sampson.

Our little team had some success that year, and we were undefeated as we headed to our last game on the schedule. It was late October, and we were playing on chilly evenings under exciting ballpark lights and having fun. I hadn't expected to get every boy a touchdown, but with one game remaining, we had only two boys left to get to score: Sampson and Maddux. By no means a charity attempt, they could both play. We simply hadn't gotten a score for them yet.

With parents and friends bundled snuggly into lawn chairs and hot chocolate fighting back the cool air, we started our last game of the year. I tried to give our boys a pep talk about working hard and giving Maddux and Sampson the same chance to score that each of them had had during the year. Our opponent was one of the better teams we had played all year, and we didn't really have control of the game until the second half. Maddux got his touchdown early in the game. In the second half, Sampson would get two or three plays and then I would hand it to one of our quicker players to try to get us a first down. After a few changes of possession and my growing anxiety about being unable to get Sampson a touchdown, we finally got a first down inside the 5-yard line. We can surely get Sampson a score with four downs and so close to the goal line. The parents were cheering encouragement loudly, and I could see Sampson's dad hoping for a Hollywood ending that I so wanted to deliver. I honestly murmured a quick prayer for a chance to make a great memory and selfishly to feel like I had done a good job.

Our opponent packed their entire team on the line of scrimmage, as a good goal line defense should, which, in my mind, legitimized our efforts. We plunge Sampson left and then right. His teammates are blocking everyone they can, and I'm proud to see each boy sweating and panting trying to come together for one of their own. I try a direct snap to Sampson for a quarterback sneak, but nothing about Sampson is sneaky. My bad call.

Finally, we face fourth down at the 1-yard line with three minutes left in the game. We dutifully take timeout and talk about each person's job and position. Logan will go on the right side of the line. I remind Jake to make a good snap and block. I tell Cole to put the ball in Sampson's belly and remind Sampson to run as fast as he can behind Logan as soon as the ball is snapped.

We break the huddle.

Jake snaps the ball.

And Sampson barrels into the end zone! He turns around to look at me, and he doesn't have the ball. He got to the line before Cole could get him the ball.

Cole turns to look at me mid play and puzzled. He deftly hops into the end zone for the score and quickly apologizes.

Deflated, I know that this was our last chance. The boys and Sampson were breathless and disappointed while I was saddened that I had failed to secure a magical Disney ending.

Strangely fortunate, the other team score on their second play, and we get the ball back. We quickly line up and throw the ball down the left side as far as a second grader can throw it. Sammy makes a great catch and immediately gets tackled. We run the same play to our tight end. Brayden catches the ball and streaks down the right sideline. Awkwardly, I'm desperately rooting for my own player to get tackled to give us a few more chances for Sampson to score. Gratefully, Brayden is tackled. We now have almost two minutes left, and we are back on our opponent's 13-yard line.

Out of creative ideas on snapping, running, or misdirection to get Sampson the ball, we again face fourth down on the 13-yard line. We had not attempted a pass to Sampson yet as that seemed only slightly more likely to succeed than cold fusion. I gave up. Everyone was getting tired and frustrated, including Sampson. This no longer felt fun, and I was starting to feel a little embarrassed that I had pushed so hard for so long.

I call a fake screen to Logan with Cole as quarterback running the ball in the opposite direction. (It isn't hard to trick eight-year-olds.) I know the misdirection will work and assume Cole will score and we would be done.

As I left the huddle, Logan quickly whispers something to Cole that I can't hear. Jake snaps the ball, Cole fakes the screen, the opposing defense chases Logan a few steps, and Cole quickly cuts to the outside the opposite direction. While a defender closes in, Cole chooses to step out of bounds at the 3-yard line, merely a foot past the first-down marker, as Logan had secretly instructed. Smarter than me. We're alive! We've got four more chances! The second-grade boys had called their own audible, finding a way to give the team more chances for Sampson.

The opposing team and crowd no longer have a sense of humor regarding my attempts to "run up the score," and they are saying not Christian things about me.

Sampson already has twelve carries in the half and is flushed and frustrated. With a collective groan, we race through three more unsuccessful plays to Sampson. Nearly completely dark, cold, and beginning to mist, our hopes for a score seem too farfetched.

Now it's our last play, fourth down and goal, in our last game of the season. This is our final effort to try to get our last kid, our Sampson, his first touchdown. The dads are out of their chairs now, simultaneously hollering their encouragement and exasperation, right at the goal line, just feet away from our huddle. The friendly midwestern farm town we're playing in is no longer friendly as their fans also gather at the goal line to urge on their defense and say mean things about my mother. A noisy scrum of parents, lawn chairs, blankets, and cups of hot chocolate have moved down the field to be closer to the action.

I tell Sampson to line up along the sideline and, after the snap, "run to the pylon and put your arms in the air."

"Pylon? The orange thing?" Sampson asks.

"Ten seconds," the referee hollers.

The last play of the last game to get our last player a touchdown—certainly Super Bowl suspense could not match this!

"Yes, the orange thing! Hurry!"

I quickly put Logan on the right side to block and tell Cole to throw it to Sampson. Jake makes a great snap. Sampson thunders into the end zone and turns around. The boys slow the advance of the defense just enough to allow Cole to throw a crisp little pass that hits Sampson square in the belly. Sampson wraps his formidable arms around the football as the referee blows the whistle and hollers "Touchdown! Game over!"

Moms explode from their lawn chairs, hot chocolate mugs launch skyward, all observing dads trading high-fives in a masculine observance of a significant life event, and the greatest dog pile in the history of youth sports ensues. The boys are so excited for the success of their teammate as I am. Sampson's dad shakes my hand as I get up from the dogpile. He has at least one tear in his eye and remarks that in thirteen years of football, including college play, he never got to touch the ball once apart from falling on a fumble.

The following spring football season, perhaps better known as baseball season to most readers, I asked Jake and Logan about their favorite plays from our season together. Jake told a favorite family story about catching the year's only Hail Mary touchdown at the end of a close game, breaking a tackle, and running into the end zone under the lights only a few steps ahead of his excited and cheering mom!

I asked Logan what his favorite play was from the season, trying to distract him from baseball. I could remember a long list of touchdowns and exciting plays. In the most profound and selfless moment of the story, Logan quietly says, "Sampson's touchdown."

There is an incredible short story in the Gospel of Luke known as the Good Samaritan. I would name it "Season's Highlight" in a current Bible version. As

Christ tells the story, listeners lean in as they recognize the road and types of travelers he describes. A man travelling on a road known to be dangerous had been attacked and left naked and unconscious. Two religious leaders of the day, more concerned with formal Jewish law and reputation than the love of others, avoided the man as they walked past. Surprisingly, a Samaritan, a despised peoples group of the day, stopped and cared for the man. Bandaging him, the Samaritan changes the entire purpose of his trip, mercifully putting the wounded man on his own donkey, leading the man to an inn, and then leaving two-days' wages for the man's care. Additionally, the Samaritan commits to return, which would have been dangerous for him to do, to follow up and pay for any remaining charges. The entire purpose of the Samaritan's trip is transformed into the sacrificial concern and practical care for another to whom he is hardly connected.

As Logan whispers "Sampson's touchdown" and Scripture trumpets our responsibility and connection to others, we must gather the courage to face the challenge of following those examples. The question that confronts me as I think of Logan and Sampson and our fun little dogpile of players is, "Am I willing to make the highlight of my season the enabling of someone else's highlight? Do I care enough for others and am I genuinely moved by their success that I consider their success my own?"

A selfless life, a life that understands the integrated connections to others, isn't without its own blessings. Jake, Logan, and Sampson continue to experience their own highlights just as they facilitated them for others. Logan was featured as a ten-year-old on a SportsCenter top ten for play in the Little League World Series and set a state high school baseball record for triples as a sophomore. Sampson is an accomplished all-American and state champion wrestler, and Jake paddles out into the Pacific Ocean alone and unafraid, having learned to surf. Those blessings become even richer when you realize that their efforts for others on their team, players to whom they were interconnected, selflessly sweating and then celebrating the victory of a friend, has helped shape their own character ahead of a lifetime of wins and losses. As a commander, it is a great honor and responsibility to try to find ways to enable the career, an award, or a season highlight for troops.

So, in simple ways, where do we start? I want to be more courageous and selfless, like the Samaritan, and more able to cherish the joy of contributing to someone else's highlight, like Logan. I want to be connected to people like this in my system where we might all benefit from that selflessness. The world needs people who endeavor to live like the lead characters of these stories.

Scripture says that the Samaritan took pity on the injured man. According to Bible scholars, some of the Greek words used in the story indicate that the Samaritan was moved deeply, and he hurt at the gut level by the vulnerability and suffering he saw. Being stirred and moved at a gut level, compelled enough to be changed, seems more difficult in a digital world that grows more isolated and less personally or physically connected. Our culture grapples with valuing and differentiating physical versus digital connection, and our lack of empathy is palpable. A University of Michigan study showed a dramatic drop in student levels of empathy. Between 1979 and 2009, student assessed empathy dropped nearly 40 percent![33] With the perpetual onslaught of news that is drawn to the tragic and outrageous, we can become either calloused or emotionally pushed beyond our capacity to respond to the genuine needs within our sphere of influence. A challenge for us is to invite our eyes to be opened to see the needs of those to whom we are connected, whether they are at work or home, at playdates or with the Saturday morning gathering of old surfers. Those needs may be big or small, serious or whimsical. Regardless, I need a heart willing to be moved deeply to be driven to action.

Another question to ask is, "Do the things that stir the heart of a loving heavenly Father routinely move and stir my heart toward compassion, empathy, and personal action?" The action step. The Samaritan stopped. He was stirred by what he saw, and then he stopped to act. He approached the unconscious man, doing so at risk of his own safety. After all, perhaps the attackers were still nearby, and as a hated minority, he exposed himself to potential accusations of causing the harm to the wounded man. The story doesn't tell us why the Samaritan was traveling along the road. Perhaps he had urgent business. Maybe he was on his way to visit family. What we do know is that the Samaritan's personal agenda was surrendered. As he stopped, he became present for the weak and vulnerable, and the intent of his trip was rewritten for a higher purpose. Yielding his agenda to care for another, without deferring to other travelers or dismissing some lack of qualifications, became the most important part of his journey.

A closing thing to note from the Samaritan's example challenges me and the quality or depth of my floundering servant leadership. Leading organizations means leading people. Leading people means walking together through life's journey, through victories and defeats. The Samaritan was personally invested in the health and recovery of the victim. He gave of his own time and his own money, and he did this freely and with no expectation of a return on his investment. Moreover, he committed to a plan of help that wouldn't conveniently resolve in a few hours. He paid for the care of the victim and promised to return some days later. The Samaritan was intentional in his intervention. He waded out into the messiness of life, embracing risk and committing to the full recovery and restoration of the victim.

I fear that in my busyness, at times, I am less a committed Good Samaritan and more of a quick triage buddy who hands someone an ice pack and tells them to hustle back into the fight. For those in my system, I want to be a bold Good Samaritan. To do the unexpected, the courageous, to be generous, or to do the patient task, which is often more difficult for me, that a servant leader would accomplish. Those to whom I am connected by leading, following, or partnering, I hope for the selflessness and confidence that, when asked what the highlight of my career was, allows me to respond, "Sampson's touchdown."

THUNDERBOLT TAKEAWAYS

- ↗ Real greatness is evident in how we care about others who can offer us nothing in return (John 15:13).
- ↗ Being cherished by friends overrides the value we may assign to the contributions or giftedness of each member. We all contribute and are connected to the health and nature of the organization (1 Corinthians 12–14).
- ↗ What erodes your personal capacity for empathy?

✗ Are you moved by the needs of others as the Samaritan was? What things in this world move you at the gut level? Will you pray with me to open our eyes to see those in need during our days?

✗ Will you stop to address the needs of others as the Samaritan did? Does the busyness of life cause you to be slow to surrender your agenda or allow you to rewrite your story for the benefit of others?

✗ Can you begin to offer your calendar to the Lord for divine appointments and spirit-orchestrated coincidences where the *primary* purpose of your day becomes someone else?

✗ Are you willing to take a risk of obedience? This life is full of broken people. Sin is messy and destructive. Yet the Lord uses broken people like you and me in service of his kingdom. How will you remain present and invest in others when personal sacrifice may be the only certain outcome?

✗ Can you grow to so focus on others that facilitating and celebrating someone else's touchdown highlight is also your own?

Muscle-flexing youth football champs.

18

NIGHT VISION

"Those who are wise shall shine like the brightness
of the sky, and those who lead the many
to righteousness, like the stars for ever and ever."
—Daniel 12:3

I remember walking across part of our tented living quarters at night in Bagram, Afghanistan, during my first deployment in May 2002. I had a LED microflashlight hooked around my dog tags to provide some light to see a path. It was the darkest place I'd ever seen. As a safety precaution, Bagram used blacked-out operations (zero overt lighting) to prevent attackers from being able to target the base, aircraft, fuel trucks, lodging camps, and so on. It was a weird sensation. I really couldn't see my hand in front of my face. As a fellow Hawg driver has said on many of our night-task force missions with no moon illumination, "It's darker than the inside of a cow out here." We would carry night-vision monocles to help us drive a little four-wheeled 'Gator' out to the jets when preparing to fly. Night-vision goggles (NVGs) and the tactics now enabled by them became an incredible advantage over our enemies.

I had been well trained to use NVGs for our flying operations, but until an unforeseen deployment to the middle of Afghanistan, we had never trained for blacked-out or covert ground operations or covert runway landings. I recall my own surprise at the night capabilities of the pilots and maintainers. As I was running my start-up checks one night, I remember pausing to look toward the jet parked next to me. Through the naked eye, I couldn't see anything of the aircraft. I could hear the engines running and only occasionally see the miners light on the crew chief's head as he was scurrying about the jet. As I would look through my goggles, I could see clear details on the jet—every light, panel, and the other pilot in his flight gear flipping through his checklists. It was startling. I would then look below the NVG field of view, and again see nothing of the jet parked only 20 yards away.

While NVGs are now common and available through any hunting or camping outfitter, the military specifications goggles continue to evolve in their fidelity and mission enhancement capability. These NVGs are black tubes that sit on a bracket in front of my eyes, attached to my flying helmet. I place the NVGs about an inch or so off of my eyes so I can choose to look through the goggles for NVG-enabled sight or under the goggles for sharp near vision and depth perception. There is a bracket inside the jet where I can store them if I take them off my helmet. In later years, I would often remove the goggles to give my aging and aching neck a break during transit portions of a sortie to and from target areas.

As a fighter pilot with a degree in psychology, my ability to understand engineering feats is nearly nonexistent. To me, these goggles are designed to work with some complex interaction of voodoo and deep black magic. The tubes themselves can magnify preexisting infrared light, light that the human eye cannot see, by converting and amplifying those photons to electrons which excite across a phospher screen. I then view the image of this conversion on a green screen, similar to how an old television used to work, complete with an eerie green glow. There is no peripheral field of view, so imagine looking at the world through two toilet paper tubes with very limited depth perception. But the goggles do amazing things with this black magic. I just click them to my helmet so they are not that complicated for me. More recently four-tube white phosphorous NVGs and infrared-capable targeting pods continue to improve the clarity, depth perception, and field of view for our warfighters, ensuring that we continue to own the night battleground.

NVGs help me see what other people cannot. When looking into a dark mountain valley, they help to answer the question, "What is really going on here?" The stars, people, buildings, vehicles, or targets that are now possible to see through the goggles are not new creations; rather, their reality has existed all along. I was aware and believed, based on my experiences, that those things existed, but staring into the dark, their precise locations, characteristics, interactions, or even purpose had not been revealed to me.

And that's what the good leaders and the purposeful people among us can do, isn't it? Visionary commanders, discerning parents, leading executives, and those wise souls among us have very similar abilities to those enabled by night vision goggles. When others stare blankly into a dark abyss and furtively shift about, what an incredible strategic advantage of wisdom (knowledge applied) exists to those who study and seek out how to view through multiple frames of experience or reading what's really going on. That advantage exists over those who can't discern what political undercurrents, personal fears, or larger purposes might be the most key and influential to a situation but occurring beyond the common and visible spectrum to most of us. What a great gift and honed advantage to see what others cannot. And that's what good leaders can do. Routinely they are sought out because they are able to see or anticipate, with better effect, variables of influence that might be shaped for desired outcomes.

The ability to cast a vision or swiftly navigate a local landscape of political or bureaucratic jungles requires someone who has trained their mind to look through the goggles and build on the lessons others have previously learned to apply. And, if we're lucky, maybe we can learn these lessons from the observations of others instead of solely through the potential pain of failure. Like the NVGs, I can choose to look through these lessons and use them as the incredible tool they are or negligently leave them stowed on a bracket and suffer the consequences.

I was paired with my flight lead, Curious, for an all-night sortie taking off from Kuwait, moving north near the Syrian border for some potential taskings before turning east toward al Samarra in Iraq near Saddam Hussein's hometown of Tikrit. We were to provide overhead firepower for a joint task force takedown and siege of an airfield and surrounding buildings. We had sectored the target area and were alternating our weapons employments of bombs, rockets, bullets, and Maverick missiles in coordination with our American and allied forces as they prepared to overrun and capture the airfield. And with our NVGs, we were able to see what was actually going on just beyond the sight of our unaided human vision.

On a sortie a few nights prior over Baghdad, it was an incredible display to see various Iraqi antiaircraft systems desperately trying to shoot an aircraft down and, in the process, revealing their own positions and weapons types with their signature visual patterns. What we witnessed were some smaller caliber weapons with high shooting rates at relatively lower altitudes up to larger systems with higher and larger detonations. Occasionally we would see unguided surface-to-air missiles streak into the sky as the enemy soldiers did not want our systems to track their positions. We also saw US firepower on display, including our own artillery and rocket systems.

After Curious and I alternated our initial bomb drops, I fired both Mavericks and both pods of highly explosive rockets at a number of different targets, each time deconflicting our weapons and jets from each other and the other aircraft or friendly troops holding their positions and awaiting the timing to overtake the airfield. While coming off a target pass and covering Curious's weapons passes, we could clearly see and identify enemy troops blindly firing their rocket-propelled grenades and assortment of weapons at the fleeting sounds of our aircraft. They couldn't see in the dark. I made multiple strafing gun passes with the 30mm GAU-8 Avenger that the A-10 is built around. Fortunate to fly a jet that could outrange and outmaneuver the enemy guns, I would fly toward the correct strafing base position and roll in on the target. The NVGs allowed me to see the muzzle flashes of the firing enemy troops. Closing on the enemy position, I placed my gun reticle directly on their firing position and was able to unleash a furious burst of cannon fire on their position. Within the cockpit, the flash of the cannon temporarily blinds pilots as the goggles now amplify our own gun fire. The glare shield and cockpit vibrate in a controlled but powerful connection to the gun as it spins within the fuselage. To those on the ground, the "monster" sounds like a mythical dragon come to life as the speed of the bullets and the spin of the gun erupt in a rapid succession of violent noise.

Turning our jets south toward Kuwait as the sun rose, I had no remaining bullets, bombs, rockets, or self-protection flares to even spit at the enemy. The airfield and base surrounding it were now under allied control, and the smoldering remnants of enemy resistance testified that our forces owned the night. We could see what others could not.

While working as an air force fellow for a Fortune 500 mobile technology company in southern California, I was fortunate to spend hours with their strategic analysis team aligned with corporate development. The depth of study and details considered—from macroeconomics to supply chain security amid global competition—was exhaustive and fascinating. Every effort made by brilliant people was an attempt to determine what was really going on and what was going to happen next and to be positioned to respond accordingly. Their efforts were analogous to what NVGs provide: the ability to see what others cannot.

But NVGs provide something else: they bring light to a dark place. In a world of cynical news cycles, global anxiety over health and wellness amid a pandemic, volatile economic markets, and political discourse that seems to relish contempt higher than collaboration, the world can begin to feel like a very dark place. Of course, it has been dark before. A desperate time of embattled hope in 1918 saw 675,000 Americans and an estimated 20 million global citizens die of the Spanish flu. Occurring during World War I, an estimated 45,000 American soldiers died of the flu while an additional 53,402 were killed due to fighting. Economic instability followed the stock market crash of 1929 when 24.8 percent and billions of dollars of market value were lost. Unable to recover from the spiral, the Great Depression ensued and saw nearly half of America's banks fail with 15 million people, about 30 percent of the workforce, unemployed.[34]

Social upheaval and mistrust of our government over civil rights and the Vietnam war during the 1960s and early 1970s brought rioting and angst that tore at the fabric of our nation.

Most critical in times of darkness are those voices and leaders with their messages and examples of hope. Hope brings the light that overcomes the darkness. Character and wisdom can propel the light of hope we are each capable of bringing. We can take back a grip of control over the darkness that confusion, sickness, and anxiety produces. Those individuals and groups most equipped to lead in dark times of crisis are those committed to digging deeply to understand what is truly going on but also able to bring a refreshing perspective that is secure in a God-given hope and purpose no matter the trials that come.

I recall flying a night mission over Iraq with a long transit time, well after we had captured Baghdad and at the outset of a lull in the violence and weapons employments of our forces. The star gazing from the cockpit, so far removed from cultural lighting and miles nearer to the stars, was absolutely stunning. When looking up with the naked eye, the number of stars and the clarity of the view was profound. And then to look through the goggles, I saw stars never before visible to my human eye leap to life as the Milky Way became clear in its outlines. It seemed as though what was merely beautiful before was now amplified ten thousand times. I looked over the canopy rail and saw the Tigris and Euphrates rivers and then again glanced at the sky just in time to see a brilliant shooting star seeming to trail comet dust that appeared to race halfway across a nation in a matter of seconds. And for a moment, I began to humbly understand that there is not a place that our Creator will not go, a darkness, history, or desperation that his presence and orchestration cannot conquer. Perhaps the inky black fingers of despair grip at each of us at times, "the night holds onto us" as a song lyric calls out. Still, the assurance exists that, when inviting an eternal God into our lives, the darkness no longer has any power over the light. With reliance on him and in cooperation with him, we can become beacons of light that will draw others through dark times.

Before the words "inspirational leader" became a byline on a book cover, the apostle Paul told the Philippians how to be the light others might need in a dark place. "Do everything without grumbling or arguing, so that you may become blameless and pure, 'children of God without fault in a warped and crooked generation.' *Then you will shine among them like stars in the sky* as you hold firmly to the word of life" (Philippians 2:14–16 NIV, emphasis added). The temptation may be to see wisdom, discernment, and the fruit of anticipation to somehow place us in a thought space that preoccupies us with the future and insulates or transports us from the difficult daily work of vocation and people. Paul was a tentmaker. Many of the disciples were fishermen. They were not those gazing, distracted, or ethereal souls who are so heavenly minded to be no earthly good. They worked. They engaged in the world. And they interacted in practical ways with the people around them.

I enjoy Mark Batterson's books. He compiled some words of the wise who have gone before us in his great book *If*. The insights help us to pair our ability to be more effective in the present while informed by a vision and understanding of what is in front of us. Batterson cites Thomas Carlyle who says, "Our main business is not to see what lies dimly at a distance, but to do what lies clearly ahead."[35] The NVGs are of little value to me as a fighter pilot if I merely stare at stars rather than maximize their use as a tool to help impact the battlefield immediately beneath me. Seeing the brilliance of what I could not see before, getting a glimpse of God's kingdom now, is meant to provide a point toward which we navigate our lives while being reassured and inspired that God is present in what goes on today. C. S. Lewis in his book *The Screwtape Letters* brilliantly encourages this by saying that God wants humankind to live and follow "to eternity itself, and to that point of time which they call the Present. For the Present is the point at which time touches eternity."[36] We are to be emboldened to make profound impacts, as stars in a dark place, to point others toward the Creator's presence and offer of salvation. Upon seeing the revelation of what only God is able to orchestrate, darkened to our human eyes, our response is to be transformed, not transfixed, as people who live by the purpose and vision of what we've seen beyond ourselves.

Using the NVGs as a metaphor for a life that pursues wisdom and discernment—a life that has the emotional intelligence to be engaged by good questions instead of threatened, to humbly lead and also courageous enough to tactfully confront shortfalls—are not skills or strategies that everyone pursues. Even those who attempt to seek wisdom, who choose to work on looking through the goggles, know that it is an acquired skill and may seem awkward, unnatural, or perhaps pointless at first. What we need, however, is to be confident, for we are assured of the fruitfulness of this discipline by wise men and women who came long before us. The book of Proverbs contains a wealth of wisdom we would be wise to consult often. One of its wise sayings is in Proverbs 20:5: "The purposes of a person's heart are deep waters, but one who has insight draws them out" (NIV). This action of drawing out requires patience and alignment.

Before my middle son's eighth-grade year, our family had made a military move to a new city. We went from a central Missouri town of less than twenty thousand people to the West Coast with an unending stream of cities from the Mexico border to north of Los Angeles. Arriving in a new state in a new city, living in a new neighborhood, preparing to go to a new middle school multiple times larger than where my son grew up, and taking an advanced English course for the first time, my son had a lot of transitions to make. I am fortunate that my family has worked to remain resilient through the changes over the years.

In the days leading up to Jake's first day of school, his anxiety was building. We made our proper preparations and attempted to slay any dragons of fear that would pop up. Prior to school starting, he needed to have read ahead for a specific book assignment. All of the local libraries were out of the book, the local military base libraries didn't have it, and all copies had been bought up from the bookstores. I was obviously a little late to this errand, and with each missed opportunity to find the book, Jake's anxiety over being behind kept building.

I continued to point out that we could simply download the book, and he could read it off of a tablet, but he refused that suggestion every time I offered it. The pinnacle of our experience was Jake's big tears that he didn't want the digital book, and my red-faced frustration that he wouldn't allow me to fix this dumb problem with an obvious answer so I could race on to the next item on the list. Far later in the story than I would like to admit, I put the goggles on and asked myself and the Lord, "What is really going on here?" Jake was scared. He had used a digital book one time before, and he didn't like it. And the stress of one more new thing where he was going to be evaluated in a new class was just one thing too much to manage. Finally, through the power of pausing and attempting to look into the dark, my attitude toward him changed from anger at what I misperceived as his stubborn obstinance to that of a dad who held and reassured his son. It was then that I found a paper copy of the book.

THUNDERBOLT TAKEAWAYS

I remember being instructed on how to get our NVGs to work properly. It was a process that precisely fine-tuned the fit and focus of our NVGs every time we flew with them. Every time. It was a routine and necessary step because of the precision of fit needed to align with our eyes and, based on a potentially different set of goggles or bracket or even our eye health, it was a fit that needed to be constantly refreshed. Likewise, the pursuit of wisdom—the patient and long view of understanding that can amplify truths before us and bring light to dark places—starts with the need for basic, routine, and daily inquiries.

↗ What is really going on here?

Creating a habit and room to pause and consider as well as inviting prayer and the wisdom of others are required if we are to learn how to peer into the dark of what we don't fully understand and build a pattern for fine-tuning our anticipation and perspectives. We will find our empathy, creative innovations, and long-term plans bear the fruit from the hard work of looking into the dark. Prayer and meditation on this question, while walking, kneeling at your bed, surfing, or driving to work all count as NVG training and exercise. This doesn't have to look like an elaborate board meeting or a hike to the top of Mount Sinai. Simply start by pausing long enough to look through the goggles, allow your eyes to adjust, and ask the question about what's really going on.

✗ Am I learning from those who have effectively done this before?

We will never be as effective at seeing in the dark if the only lessons we are willing to learn are experiential. Those who love us or follow us deserve for us to take our role seriously and to be spared the time and pain of only learning straight through the nose. We need to look to sources outside of ourselves for the wisdom we need. We can learn from strategic thought leaders from the corporate world, the ancient wisdom of Proverbs, practical insights of a battle-tested military commander, and many other reliable sources.

✗ Am I transformed by what is revealed to me?

Do not be conformed to this age, but be transformed by the renewing of the mind, so that you may discern what is the will of God— what is good and acceptable and perfect. (Romans 12:2)

I am convinced that the Lord expects us to be different in how we live, to be transformed by our encounter with him and the wisdom that comes from seeing life through personal goggles that are affixed to an eternal perspective. It is not enough to simply be aware of what is good and acceptable or what strategic long win may be evident through study. The most critical aspect of this process is to allow our very nature, our thought patterns and views, to be weighed, sifted, and eventually transformed through an immersion in Scripture and desire for growth. This transformation is what enables our ability to become light in a dark place.

Night vision goggles also help us to find our way to safety. Landing under covert conditions, looking through the goggles with a limited field of view and poor depth perception, were new to me as a lieutenant in Afghanistan. Our innovative method of NVG landings was to get a radar approach down through the towering bowl of mountains, guiding us back to the airfield. We were given precise heading and altitude directions as we descended toward the runway. Depending on the weather and blowing dust, we would eventually pick up the temporary covert glow sticks that had been dropped at intervals down the sides of the runway. With such limited fields of view, I would tend to try to level the jet for an instant at 10 feet to quickly look down over both sides of the canopy rail to be sure there was some concrete underneath me and then gratefully slam the jet onto the ground.

More than making us more lethal, the goggles also ensure we make it back home safely—in this life and the next.

So we do not lose heart. . . . We look not at what can be seen but at what cannot be seen, for what can be seen is temporary, but what cannot be seen is eternal.
—2 Corinthians 4:16-18

Night vision goggle training.

19

WHY FIGHTER PILOTS WIN

*"I heard the bullets whistle, and, believe me,
there is something charming in the sound."*
–George Washington

"Who's coming in second?"
**–Larry Bird to the other all-star competitors prior to winning
his third consecutive three-point contest in 1988**

*"I have fought the good fight, I have finished the race;
I have kept the faith."*
–Paul (2 Timothy 4:7)

*T*he sun was starting to set. Each time my jet circled toward the west, my peripheral vision would pick up the growing orange and red glow now lighting the sky. I and my wingman were tracking a target set of known enemy fighters while their identities, pattern of life, and the authorization to strike were under evaluation. We circled silently above, like patient sharks waiting, rehearsing, preparing to fire newly minted laser guided rockets. These rockets are a uniquely lethal and low collateral damage weapon based on the speed of the rocket at target impact and the very small warhead. Obsessively concerned about removing any potential collateral damage, this small and fast rocket mitigated the potential negative weapon impact effects to nearly zero. The A-10 was now a platform that allowed fighter pilots to become airborne snipers with the precision of a weapon to strike a single target from a few miles away while anything merely feet away could remain unharmed. Neither of us had fired this specialized rocket as yet, but its capabilities had been proven from use in Syria and had been employed off of multiple airframes.

We had trained our aircraft geometry to enable one aircraft to fire the rocket while the other jet maintained a clear laser spot and field of fire. We had rehearsed the specific and crisp communication between ourselves and had practiced precise laser tracking on dynamic moving targets for a year prior to this moment. Decades of military flying and deployments and all the previous hits and misses and debriefs helped shape the opportunity for us to be at our best in the moments that would matter the most.

I have referenced the apostle Paul and his courageous commitment to the power and universal truths of Christ and Scripture. Writing from what I imagine to be a dark and damp prison cell in Rome and knowing his death was imminent, Paul took a moment to reflect after exhorting Timothy to give his best for the kingdom of God. In one simple verse, informed by a lifetime of experience, Paul summarized his noble life of service as one involving his fight for the highest purposes, his own perseverance of running a race, and the sustaining vision and energy of keeping the faith. As he said, "I have fought the good fight; I have finished the race; I have kept the faith."

Paul's clarity and reflection occurred on the doorstep of his own death. To our benefit is the chance to consider perhaps early in the first quarter of our lives, at halftime, or between seasons of change, if we are emboldened to be at our best because our cause is worthy of a good fight. Are we disciplined to persevere as a runner in a race? Do we believe and live as if our faith of a greater love and greater reward await us?

A key misperception is that the great and valiant battles of this world, the battles that promote courage over fear, hope over despair, health over sickness, and mercy to the brokenhearted, are skillfully fought only by those on the grandest stage, in the midst of the most epic of circumstances, and serving in the most popularized vocations. When our hearts invite room for the presence and wisdom of the supernatural Creator, and we offer him the baton to conduct the events of our lives, the job titles our culture values, like fighter pilot, CEO, professor, pastor, or doctor, become merely instruments by which his love might be communicated. The excellent performance of our roles is our duty—yours and mine—and every station in life becomes our personalized platform by which we are called to boldly confront racism, prejudice, and injustice, and to protect and nurture the most vulnerable among us. Each of us have a platform to convey God's love, independent of our education, income, tribe, or nation. Each of us is purposed to be an instrument designed in *his* image and charged with filling *his* purpose.

The Lord wants to work his eternal purposes, woven through every compartment of your life and through your fingers, into your own workplace, relationships, and neighborhood. There is a godly nobility to work and being diligent in honoring the Lord exactly where you are today. Whether confined to a wheelchair, driving a truck, teaching young children how to pronounce their letters, or leading a company of thousands, our Savior has a role for us to warmly embrace and run to fulfill. That's why, when we look at why fighter pilots win, the key tenants apply universally to whatever your hand has chosen to do and in whatever place you are planted. Be it leading neighborhood playdates, working in a construction yard, or sitting through teleconferences from your kitchen while still in your pajamas, who we are and what we do matter. So Paul tells us: "Whatever task you must do, work as if your soul depends on it, as for the Lord and not for humans, since you know that from the Lord you will receive the inheritance as your reward; you serve the Lord Christ" (Colossians 3:23–24). We may have human employers, but all of us ultimately work for one Lord—Jesus Christ. And that gives any work we do its supreme significance and meaning.

The environmental factors of Afghanistan seem especially able to confound perfect laser aimpoint. Constant challenges regarding the time of day, temperature contrasts, shadows, trees, and the unpredictable route of a target required perpetual attention. Changing one variable would require us to reassess the potential shot windows while considering clusters of high walled compounds, our relative position in the sky, sun reflectivity, camera focus, light or dark contrasts of looking through the targeting pod, and considering what might be the best angle of attack.

In one radio call, our adrenalin snaps us from disciplined rehearsals to knowing this is the moment to execute. "Hawg 55, Trinity 06 has approved this target." At some point later in my career, I began murmuring to myself a line from the movie *The Patriot* when leaving a hold for a target strike: "Lord, make me fast and accurate."[37] My wingman was already holding to the southwest. The target turned west down the road we had previously chosen as a shot window. I lagged the target's turn a bit south and then turned toward them, flying above and behind their left shoulder. I adjusted the laser spot a foot more forward on the moving target. My wingman confirmed he had good laser energy return, meaning the rocket should guide to our desired impact point. "Pistol, 12 seconds," he called. The rocket was in the air. It was my job to guide it to impact as the target accelerated west along a canal.

I had employed weapons countless times before this occasion. But my heart still pounded with a fighter pilot's version of buck fever each time given the sober and dynamic nature of the mission. I had not yet seen this weapon work, so I was not yet an experienced believer in it. I was also now the squadron commander. Clowning up the cockpit with errors certainly would not do well for me to lead by example.

Twelve seconds to wait for impact can seem like an eternity. And the impact was spectacularly violent, precise, and surgically contained. It was flawlessly lethal less than forty-five seconds after the target was approved. Given all of the variables, rarely does a mission task go so cleanly. I became a new believer in the weapon and pleased for such a pure mission to help kick off our deployment. Our deployed team, including the maintainers, intelligence and weather briefers, bomb loaders, and medical and support members could be proud of how quickly they had showed up in an unplanned place and made a difference in less than a day. Not every shot goes as well, and we learn a lot from our misses, but it felt great to help start this deployment off with a win.

Fight the Good Fight

One reason fighter pilots win is that, when called to fight, we rise to the occasion and boldly run toward the sound of the guns. Not in a twisted view of bloodthirst, but as a very human response to the nature of God imprinted on our lives. There is no greater love than to place ourselves in harm's way, potentially to die, for another. Be it physical danger, a sacrifice of time or money, being completely present for another, protecting those precious and vulnerable, or an issue of good over evil playing itself out in our community, our hearts must be moved and our purposes declared when we need to be at our best when it matters the most. There are battles worthy of our best, most often in the service of others and for principles greater than our own comfort. We are charged to be *bold* in confronting them. And bold does not mean we know how everything will resolve; we simply know that deep within our human nature and through our connection to others something is driving us to take some quick first steps toward the battle. Rather than choosing to leave the matter or hardship for someone else to serve, we step out of the crowd, as King David did when only a lowly shepherd, and point our finger at the Goliath of what is wicked and say, "How dare you!"

I have witnessed my kind and diminutive wife boldly wade right into the middle of the lives of single moms and paroled dads whose history of drugs, jail, and bad choices dared to compromise the future and safety of their precious kids. She pours out her life, her treasure, her time and heart with no promise of a return on the investment. Brushing right past her own fears, heartaches, and uncertainties, she remains unwilling to defer to someone "better" who has yet to show up. The calling to engage the battles around us have nothing to do with our personality or job or how aggressive we may be. Your unique platform and position, skills and calling can fill a role in the battles around you.

There are fights worthy of our best. The performance expectations among our nation's finest warriors are exceptionally high. There is no dilution of the high standards, there is no career achievement award or free pass that allows them to return to combat unproven. We each fly routine check rides and are periodically evaluated in the simulator for mission and instrument proficiency and knowledge. And these warriors are certified as combat mission ready, which is a different certification than being without flaw or need of improvement.

When I walk up to my jet, ready to fly for the day, I exchange a pleasant salute and greeting from the crew chief, who is going to loan me his aircraft for a few hours. He hands me a large binder of forms. The binder is cared for but well worn, and it contains all the data about the daily health of the jet. It lists who flew it last and for how long, how many hours the jet has flown that week, and then lists all repairs or pending maintenance. The pending maintenance mentioned can be very minor, like a paint chip, or routine, like a fuel or oil sample, or include a "Red X," meaning that critical work must be accomplished before the jet can fly again. But for twenty-three years, the jet given to me was almost always flyable though not perfect. There were often flaws and repairs pending, which were always attended to by the hands of an expert.

The mission of the kingdom of God needs us now. The enemy will not wait for us to be perfect before he attacks. And frankly, those of us in harms way do not care if there is a paint chip in our life. We are needed now.

As brothers and sisters in service of Christ, I implore you not to wait for a perfection that will not occur on this side of heaven. Rather, determine if you are flyable, can you get airborne, and serve the mission today. Is there a youngster in your classroom who needs to simply be greeted with joy and made to feel special, or a coworker who might need to be lovingly called into account for his or her words or demeanor? Perhaps there's a family member who needs from you prayer and fasting so that person might return to the Lord. Or maybe you know a solitary and grumpy neighbor who would be blessed to share smores over a fire pit with your family. You are uniquely positioned right now. You do not need to be someone new or go someplace new to make an impact for Jesus. Given your relationships, language, culture, geography, or expertise, there is a mission uniquely tailored for your skill set that only you, not our nation's elite warriors, can make. While it's true that we all remain a work in progress until Christ returns (Philippians 1:6), we need you to get airborne today, right where you live.

And as you live and work for Christ, heed Paul's exhortation to the Philippians: "Live your life in a manner worthy of the gospel of Christ, so that, whether I come and see you or am absent and hear about you, I will know that you are standing firm in one spirit, striving side by side with one mind for the faith of the gospel and in no way frightened by those opposing you" (Philippians 1:27–28).

Finish the Race

There is not a more competitive group of people in the world than a squadron of fighter pilots at a go cart track, paintball outing, whitewater rafting, or competitive strafing on the bombing range. And I love it! Creative cheating is not only tolerated but encouraged. It is a nuanced and ever shifting line of what is acceptable, but we all know when the line has been crossed. Our Christmas party even involves a timed and full contact gift exchange. I actually drove a fellow pilot from the Christmas party to the ER for stitches a number of years ago. This competitive spirit is part of what drives fighter pilots to win. It's also the case that fighter pilots win because they quickly identify that winning, with whatever situation has been dealt, is most often the objective.

As a fighter pilot, I immediately connect with Paul's comment that he has been in a race and has now finished it. The race as a metaphor for faith and life threads throughout his writing. He even says in one place, "Do you not know that in a race the runners all compete, but only one receives the prize? Run in such a way that you may win it" (1 Corinthians 9:24). Don't show up hoping you will be impressively mediocre. Instead, give the effort and strategy and attitude needed to win. A win might be a perfect weapons delivery, the score of a competing team, a solid inspection or exercise result, or minimizing the effort needed to accomplish an ancillary task. In my vocation, the single-mindedness of winning and the cost associated with losing create a ruthless and near innate disposition to get rid of any weight, hindrance, or distraction that slows our ability to run and win. This narrowing of focus can also quickly offend. You can't run fast without getting rid of competing agendas that dilute resources and confuse priorities. You also can't run with perseverance at a great distance alone, so communicating a clear vision of where we're running, why it's important to win, and empowering others to creatively shed even sacred unnecessary ballast, even if it hurts some feelings, can help us to accelerate.

Last summer I had the chance to spend some time chasing a bucket-list item. I've always wanted to learn to surf. Renting a home near the beach for a one-year family adventure gave me the chance to try. And did I ever try. I would paddle out as hard as I could into the crashing foam of the Pacific Ocean, snorting and wheezing and trying to count twenty strokes as my shoulders quivered with exhaustion. I would then turn around and try to catch a wave, inevitably having the wave crash on my back and throw me around like a washing machine, turning me upside down and bouncing me off the ocean floor until I would gasp for air and paddle out again. I noticed the other surfers effortlessly sitting on their boards, enjoying the beautiful views and solace of the ocean as I would gasp past them as though in football two-a-day practices. I was red-faced and exhausted. I got up early each morning and excitedly raced down to the water and plunged forward head first into the waiting waves, sure that effort and athletic ability that I may have had in the 1990s would carry me.

I would ask the surfers questions but not practice exactly what they said. Even my neighbor, with a garage full of forty years of surfing trophies, told me I needed a board that didn't have the fin broken off and to stay in the foam longer to learn to stand up. After one exhausting session where my frustration actually began to show and where I continually got flipped over by wave after wave, I walked in to sit by my wife who was quietly reading a book. She looked at me after watching the spectacle and said, "Well, that ought to loosen up your back."

For a month, I, who know better, did not study anything about surfing. I didn't even watch a single YouTube video on how to stand up on a surfboard. Day after day I hit the water to master a craft I knew very little about. Even when I would lean over my dinner plate and saltwater would pour from my nose, I still didn't give in to learning more about surfing before trying to ride a wave. In my mind, there was no time or need for study. I just wanted to get out there and do it!

I wasted an entire month of my precious ten months by the ocean because I didn't think to watch a four-minute YouTube video. After I finally watched it, I could stand up in relative moments compared to the time I had wasted. It took another three weeks for me to watch the second video, which ran only two minutes, on how to paddle to catch a wave properly. This was also transformative to my naïve understanding. Six weeks later, I could finally paddle and barely stand up, but there were more lessons to learn.

I had bought a heavy foam training surfboard designed to be stable and soft for all of the times I would bounce my head off of it. On one particularly "big" day when the surf was especially ornery, I paddled and gasped and fought out into the water. A few rides into the day, I popped up on the board and felt my big toe get caught in the leash. There was a slip knot in the rubberized tubing of the leash that I hadn't paid attention to at the start of the day. As I tumbled off a big wave, the water slammed the heavy board down and away from me, clamping the knot closed around my big toe and pulling me under in excruciating pain. I came up out of the water praying and swearing as a second wave slammed onto the board and pulled me under the water. I flailed my arms around trying to grab the leash. I was convinced I was about to lose my toe or, alternatively, die the most undignified death, drowning by my big toe. I eventually got hold of the leash and loosened the knot. Finally out of the water, I limped home with a toe that didn't look or work properly for the next few weeks. This taught me to check the leash on my board.

Each situation we encounter, each race in which we enter, deserves its own specialized study and attention to detail. To finish a race requires perseverance, consistency, and knowledge. Leaning only on pure effort or exuberance that outpaces diligent education is sure to result in the undignified death by big toe drowning. It may give you an impressively swift start to the race, but you will subsequently miss turns and create more havoc than good. Prior successes or failing to get the right expert's opinion for that exact race, complete with its own intricacies, not only won't lead to victory but might even hold us back from even reaching the finish line. We've all seen races where someone jumps out to a very aggressive lead and then runs out of the energy needed to maintain the lead. Our behavior at home or in the workplace is not much different. Can we then blend passion, study, grit, and wisdom to be at our best as a mom or dad, friend, fighter pilot, parent, or pastor?

Another big-toe lesson is to strive after that strange paradoxical nature that has the confidence and calling to be bold yet also humble enough to realize we've never fully arrived. Regardless of who you have led, jets flown, articles published, mergers facilitated, or how many noses you have wiped, there are always opportunities to be a joyful newcomer who just wants to plunge into something new. I hope to be as my children when toddlers at the park, more delighted to be learning and active than embarrassed by falling down. And those toddlers, at their best moments, do not carry the the hubris of self-sufficiency that can infect each of us. The sin of self-sufficiency displaces our commitment to growth, inviting the wisdom of others, and finding humility.

There are plenty of days that I would rather be able to depend on myself than on the Lord. I would prefer to get what I want at the exact moment I want it rather than rely on an unseen and supernatural Savior. In reality, I'm conning myself into thinking that I can control the timelines and outcomes and then take the credit for job accomplished. However, I have learned what happens when I rely solely on my overestimated wit or work ethic for an extended season. I become exhausted, lonely, and frustrated, and I despair as to my purpose and capabilities. But when my connection and dependence on God becomes the source of my energy and refreshment, my burden weighs far less for two are carrying the weight, and he can handle far more and in a better way than I can.

That said, I also acknowledge that I have been fortunate to work with some of the most talented people in the country. From many of them I have seen that self-reliance can, indeed, result in many levels of worldly success. But for even the most gifted, who look only to themselves for truth and solutions, their profit is hollow. They may have gained the world of their desires, but they are also surrounded by the carnage and collateral damage of those around them who are aware of how unnecessary they have become. So the success they savor, they savor alone. The blessing of a daily humility that seeks mercies, grace, or wisdom to be new each morning from the Lord acknowledges that we alone are not the solution. Rather, I alone am quite often the start of my problems.

So while all of us should run the race of life to finish it and win it, we should not try to run it alone.

Keep the Faith

Paul concludes his comments to Timothy, sounding like he has written the closing statement of his own obituary, that he had "kept the faith." Faith is what connects our hopes and sense of purpose. It is the assurance and hope for something yet unseen (Hebrews 11:1). Paul is talking about his life calling of evangelism and making disciples, that in spite of every conceivable obstacle, he never lost sight of his purpose and calling. Although it may sound obvious, there are many who arrive at some point in their career and ask, "Why am I doing this again? What about this stirred me so deeply that I chose to get into it in the first place?"

I had a massive shoulder reconstruction a few years ago. Over the years, I've had six sports injury-related surgeries. You would think I would have some great stories of athletic glory to go with that number of operations. I don't. I had two shoulder surgeries in college, and I never properly rehabilitated as I should have. Over the course of my next twenty years of flying, I became accustomed to compensating, protecting, or ignoring the health of my shoulder. After a familiar "pop" in the gym one day, my strength in the arm began to fail over the next months. I was in significant pain and losing some feeling in my fingers. A contrast MRI was inconclusive, but the nerve test showed some impingement. The nerve test made me want to cry. A soft-spoken nerve specialist, with what I can only describe as a clinically deranged affinity for torture, stuck small pins in my hand, wrist, and arm and then shocked me with an electrified probe. Supposedly this measured how fast the electrical pulse traveled through my nerves. I did confess I would tell him whatever he wanted to know about military secrets to please make it stop. At this point in medical history and advancement, this is the best idea we have— pins and an electrical probe?

Some weeks later, I entered the office of my gifted surgeon, Dr. Jay Rapley, the day after my third shoulder reconstruction surgery but the first by Dr. Rapley. I remember his words clearly: "That was in the top four worst shoulders I've ever seen. That looked like a bomb had gone off in there."

Even while recovering from the surgery and foggy with a lack of sleep and pain medication, my competitive nature caused me to smirk as I thought, *Top four? That's pretty good.* My wife rolled her eyes on cue as she saw me smile.

Dr. Rapley continued: "The rotator cuff was torn nearly in two with muscle and ligament damage. I had to shave bone to make a channel for your nerve. The muscle in your shoulder and arm hasn't fired properly in years. You've got nothing left back there. If you tear this one out, we're looking at a replacement."

I learned in the following six months of difficult rehab that the weakness and atrophy I had conveniently ignored and was too busy to address for twenty years had devastating effects that, despite the magic of healing and the work of a phenomenal surgeon, could not be completely overcome.

Faith is the nerve that needs to be allowed to fire without obstruction in our lives. A grounding in the truth of Scripture "fires," or communicates, clearly to us on a daily basis to our own humanity and to our calling to serve a purpose higher than our own comfort. That faith is what can sustain us and compel us to press through hardship when life becomes dark. As a refined instrument that requires daily calibration for perfect function, we also need to plug in daily for a routine "re-caging" of what motivates our hearts, the purposes we serve, and the callings we embrace. Just as aviation instruments like gyroscopes and inertial navigation systems drift and lose accuracy over time and require routine updates or corrections to be "re-caged," so do the motives of our hearts. The stress and monotony of daily life, and the continued overlapping of home and work, school and activities can begin to blur our vision and suffocate our lungs from life-giving energy that comes with doing what we are called to do. Without a properly firing sense of faith, much like a firing nerve, that delivers a coherent and consistent purpose and value through every area of our lives, we will inevitably experience atrophy and confusion. We can even become accustomed to the damage we have done and unaware of the cumulative effects, just as I had done with my shoulder.

Faith is the story of hope and nourishment of our own souls. From a holistic view, who we are, what we do, and whom we connect with provide the fabric of our lives. While the corporate setting fights to provide employees with purposeful and meaningful work in an attempt to connect the souls of their employees to their work and productivity, the Gospel of Mark provided the same fiscal forecast long before. In this Gospel, Jesus asks, "What good is it for someone to gain the whole world, yet forfeit their soul?" (Mark 8:36 NIV). Profit, gain, winning, or success are not innately bad. Rather, the corporate world, Christian ministries and charities, and even parents of children who fail to launch all inherently understand the same thing: Without routine connection to purpose, meaning, and calling, our lives, motivations, and success become as garbage, as Paul has said (Philipians 3:1–10), and the condition of our soul begins to atrophy. In contrast, the growing realization that our life is a race to be run with daily endurance and a humble and daily attention to nurturing our souls changes our view of life from a splashy gallery of epic highlights to a testament of simply and diligently stepping to the next stone on our path.

I have been fortunate to experience many highlights, and I expect your stories, which I hope this book have triggered, reflect the handwriting of a loving God through each retelling. Epic events are great to reflect upon, and they help urge us along when the path gets lonely or difficult. I have been fortunate to fly into sunrises and sunsets over the Atlantic and the Pacific, to have dogfought F-18s from Finland, to have landed at places that aren't officially places, to have parachuted with green berets, to have flown faster than the speed of sound, to have killed bad guys and helped rescue some good guys. I've seen my three children born, coached Little League, swam with sharks, stayed in a fourteenth-century castle with my wife, and raced an Audi A-6 on the Autobahn in Germany. I have briefed senators, met an ambassador, tactfully disagreed with four-star generals, been hugged by an Afghan warlord, floored the accelerator on a Ferrari, and chased giraffes from a jeep in Kenya. As I type these things, they may read as epic events. To me, though, they are a fun recollection of what the Lord has humbly allowed me to do while hoping to honor him. All of these things are meaningless garbage if they cost me my faith and relationship with those I love. And to win in the mission assigned to us for individual purpose, meaning, and calling requires us to be rid of any weight no matter how epic. Anything that compromises our faith and family or distracts us from serving for a greater reward is dead weight, worthy only for the garbage bin.

THUNDERBOLT TAKEAWAYS

Executive coaches and frontline managers around the world have likely done the write-your-own obituary exercise as a means of helping their clients or coworkers gain a sense of their own values and to provide a life vision to strive after. As we've seen, the apostle Paul has provided us the perfect outline for this exercise to help us forge a life in which there is an interwoven coherence of grace, love, and courage that connects our work, relationships, and our well-being. It is our opportunity to enter a good fight and run our race so to win.

- ✗ Fighter pilots are in the fight, fully. This is the core of what their call and training is about.

What has been placed in your life that is worthy of a fight? What person, cause, or noble battle needs what the Lord can provide uniquely through you?

✗ Fighter pilots serve with courage for others and for their country and cause.

Has intimidation, complacency, or fear frozen you from action? Have cultural norms or pressures moved you to be silent when your voice and perspective are as valuable as ever?

Sometimes we're reluctant to boldly step out and engage the battle that compels us because we can't see very far down the path and we're unsure what our final destination is. We may be convinced that taking the first step is the right thing to do to engage the need in front of us, but uncertainty as to what is step five or step ten prevents even our noble stride to step one. Are you still running the race to win? Or have the burdens of anxiety, fatigue, a fear of missing out, or brokenheartedness become too heavy and caused you to simply hope to survive rather than be energized and driven as for a prize?

On the professional cycling circuit, the Tour de France is a twenty-one-stage race occurring over a twenty-three-day period and covering 2,200 miles. It's a grueling race, requiring the utmost in dogged persistence and focus.

In our life's race, we may feel at times as if it consists more of a rise-and-grind drudgery than anything else. But in reality, each stage challenges something new in us, possibly in an area of weakness or an area of strength. The race is comprised of much more than a finale, great deeds, and epic events heading toward victory or defeat. Rather, as sustained and led by the Spirit, our function is to live countless great stages and seasons as coherent chapters of the grand race of life that we run to win.

✗ Is the faith of your heart, your purpose, your impact, and your meaning clearly seen weaving through every area of your life? Are you able to keep that faith at the forefront of what you do? Or has your life been reduced to a list of tasks or a paycheck? Do you need to confront a now boundaryless overlap of work and life that saps your energy or initiative, blurs your focus, and dilutes your sense of calling?

Some professional cyclists prefer the hill climbs, others the short sprints. Some riders thrive amid the peloton while others excel in individual riding. Life will present seasons that seem perfectly suited to our skills and preferences while other steps may seem like desolate seasons of punitive hill climbs. Winners know that these stages are part of the race. And the only way to finish the race and win it is to keep on pedaling.

A-10 low-angle strafe. It feels like winning.
(Tommy Davis / Instagram @tommyd_photography)

20

"MY DADDY KILLS BAD GUYS"

*"Blessed be the Lord my Rock, who trains my hands
for war and my fingers for battle."*
—David (Psalm 144.1)

 strange title, I know.

I imagine the innocence and trust of a child calling out "daddy" as he or she takes comfort simply at saying the word. The young ones are confident in the protection and love that will respond.

The word "kills" shifts the sentence from something warm and safe to something that shocks with feelings of fright or danger.

The seeming complete mismatch of "daddy" and "kills" held my attention as I stood in a grade school hallway. Sarah and I were attending a parent-teacher conference at the elementary school. Colorful construction paper artwork dripping with too much glue decorated the drab hallways.

As we came to my son's class, their assignment had been to write about a hero in their life and to draw an accompanying picture. His essay was a touching tribute to me as he wrote about the protection I helped provide to keep him and his friends safe. He also wrote about how surprised he was at how silly grown-up pilots acted. He had seen a Rock 'em Sock 'em Robots game near the pilots' kitchen, and watched the pilots eat Jalapeño popcorn for breakfast and play arcade games in our squadron bar.

Then I looked at Jake's picture accompanying the essay. He had drawn a bubble winged A-10 rolling out of the sky and shooting at bad guys on the ground. At the top of the paper he wrote, "My Daddy Kills Bad Guys." I laughed with a quick pride that he was repeating what I told him and that there was no deference to political correctness in his little body. And then I wondered, *What in the world did his teacher think?* Or worse, as I laughed out loud, *What did the very young student teacher from the local college think was going on in our house?* As parents, we often delight and occasionally gasp when our kids freely express their thoughts.

My wife worked as a speech pathologist for the schools. I had coached both of my older kids for a few years, made a few pop-in lunches a year, and always came to the Veteran's Day ceremony. Living in a small military town, we knew the schools and the other families, and there was a great respect for the military. But I imagined my son's picture brought a strange incongruity to any teacher's eye who tried to envision how a loving family might also have a parent so callously trained to be a killer. The idea that the jets that circled over the town were just practicing flying was a lot more comfortable than the idea that those jets were actually training to be more lethal in their use.

In the first days of my air force flying training, the word "compartmentalization" was introduced. The theory is that, with practice, each area of our lives could be blocked off from the other areas so that any personal challenges, weariness, or worries would not follow us into the cockpit or workplace and affect our ability to do the mission. I have always believed that we are capable of narrowing our focus for periods of time and being fully present, which you absolutely must be in my occupation. I'm sure my understanding was incomplete as a young lieutenant, but it seemed as though the best pilots were expected to create impermeable boundaries between their work life and their other life and that those barriers might even require reinforcement to ensure there was never any visible bleed over.

The truth is, no matter our role in life, being fully present in our service, tasks, or conversations requires a sacrifice and effort that might actually bear the greatest fruit in someone else's life. I have never really believed in compartmentalization. I was raised to understand that all that I am and all that I do and those with whom I live are part of an interwoven and connected fabric. Consistent threads of faith were woven into my life that communicated to me that I am a valuable child of the King, I am created for a purpose, I am an incomplete work, and I need to consider others as more valuable than myself. Those threads then tie the decisions I make, with my finger on the trigger, to the same values that understand that I need to be trustworthy and that there are occasions when going in harm's way for another is the greatest possible honor and calling.

The Department of Defense has matured a great deal over the last two plus decades, realizing that for their members to be at their best, at the razor's edge of optimal mission performance, a holistic view of well-being is the building block for a long term healthy and thriving military unit. The DOD's initiatives in regard to resiliency, well-being, suicide awareness, mutual support, sexual assault prevention, and fostering a culture of respect and trust have been noble. The time, money, and research spent on caring for our troops and their families announces that their health and value are defined by more than what they can simply produce.

We human beings weren't designed to attempt to cut up areas of our lives and bounce from one stand-alone life compartment to some other quarantined area we only encounter on the occasional weekend or holiday. As a commander, I often saw the confusion, embarrassment, and dysfunction that results for a service member when one area of their life breaks through an artificial and overstressed barrier and flows over the walls into every other area. These troops are profusely apologetic and uncertain how their hardships will be viewed or supported. As a military member or as parents or supervisors, we need to recognize the holistic nature of our own health and that of others. And when work-life boundaries blur, we must realize that life can be messy, overlapping, interconnected, and rewarding, and it isn't likely to fit in small, self-contained boxes.

I am never more present, narrowed, or engaged than on the eight seconds of a weapons pass. But then I turn and fly home and notice the picture of my family on the back of my knee board. There will always be a need and benefit to being able to truly narrow our focus while allowing our spiritual life to feed the meaning and purpose of our work and relationships. My hope is for each of you to courageously strive toward an interconnected life of purpose, health, and well-being with consistent threads of faith and values sewing together the areas of your life that matter the most: faith, family, and purpose. I hope these stories have encouraged your own retellings, your own stories of faith and valor, success and failure, and that you have been able to see the daily hand-writing of a living God in your life. I pray that these words of encouragement touch your life, whether a veteran, a bored Christian, a spiritual seeker, or a lonely heart, and that they help you to know that God sees you, desires to know you, and wants you to know him well.

Only an interconnected life can then make sense of the sentence, "My daddy kills bad guys."

THUNDERBOLT TAKEAWAYS

- ◢ We are called to a living faith in a world that is broken and lost.
- ◢ We are designed to live this life in deep connection with others, committed to leading and loving more like Christ each day.
- ◢ Pursuing our purpose, being grounded in Scripture, learning from experts, empowering truth-tellers, and running to win also ask us to courageously grapple with areas of our life that are in need of repentance and refinement.
- ◢ We are asked to do hard things because we love Christ more than our own comfort or safety.
- ◢ We are called to live a life of self-sacrifice, not self-focus.
- ◢ Christ was sent out for us. We are sent for others. How might you be sent and used for the kingdom today?

Attack!
(Tommy Davis / Instagram @tommyd_photography)

ACKNOWLEDGMENTS

To the author and finisher of my faith, thank you Jesus for bringing purpose and coherence in a world that is both beautiful and broken.

I thank my children—Jenna, Jake, and Trevor—whose childhoods were different from the other kids but who have thrived writing their own exciting stories with Christ and who have been faithful and positive when things have been hard, new, or scary. You are more important to me than any phone call, sortie, or day at work.

To my parents, Dr. Brad and Judy Riddle, who provided a foundation of love, faith, and permission to jump! Dad, thank you for your expert biblical and counseling insights you provided as such critical contributions to this book.

To my brother and best friend, Dr. Eric Riddle, thank you for the great comedic material and, more importantly, living a life of service and sacrifice.

To my sister Bethany who has lived a lifetime example of grit, grace, and loud laughter.

To my friend Yeti. I miss you. No one lived life to the full more than you. Thank you for taking us along with you.

I appreciate my patient and persistent mentor, Les Kletke, discoverable as "Les, the Book Coach" whose humor and practical insights made our conversations something to enjoy.

And to Bill Watkins, my editor, I appreciate your military service and your generosity of time, wisdom, and sincere interest in *Faith, Family and Fighter Jets*.

To the men and women of the WGFS, I could not be more humbled and indebted than to have shared our lives together. Seriously.

ABOUT THE AUTHOR

Colonel Todd "Riddler" Riddle is a combat decorated fighter pilot, battle-tested fighter squadron commander, former 82nd Airborne parachutist, and youth pastor. "Riddler" recently served as a Secretary of Defense Executive Fellow with a Fortune 500 global communications company supporting executive vice-president-level decision making ranging from artificial intelligence chip design to business development and military applications of 5G-edge technologies. While also serving as a top ranked national speaker on resilience and well-being, Riddler has drawn from his time in ministry and as a collegiate teaching fellow to support the US Department of Defense Yellow Ribbon program as a nationally top-rated keynote speaker. Colonel Riddle and his family live near Washington, DC, while his current military duty is at the Pentagon.

ENDNOTES

1   I'm referring to the three hundred maintainers for a deployed squadron—those who keep the jets flying—crew chiefs, bomb loaders, avionics, engine mechanics, sheet metal specialists, and so many more. These are the enlisted backbone and soul of a flying unit.

2   To learn more about William Wilberforce, see Eric Metaxas, *Amazing Grace: William Wilberforce and the Heroic Campaign to End Slavery* (New York: HarperCollins, 2007) and John Pollock, *Wilberforce* (Belleville, MI: Lion Publishing, 1977). For shorter summaries of Wilberforce's life, see James Emery White, *Serious Times: Making Your Life Matter in an Urgent Day* (Downers Grove, IL: InterVarsity Press, 2004), chap. 1, "The Second Fall: A Hero for Humanity: The Life of William Wilberforce"; John C. Pollock, "William Wilberforce and the Abolition of Slavery," in *Great Leaders of the Christian Church*, ed. John D. Woodbridge (Chicago, IL: Moody Press, 1988), 301–305; and *Encyclopedia Britannica* online, s.v. "William Wilberforce," https://www.britannica.com/biography/William-Wilberforce.

3   This quote comes from C. S. Lewis's book *The Screwtape Letters* (New York: HarperSanFrancisco, 1996), letter 12, p. 60. The words come from a demon named Screwtape who says that he heard them uttered by one of the "patients"—a human being—upon his arrival to hell.

4   For a discussion of the varieties of the quotation and who may have said what, see "Dance Like Nobody's Watching," Quote Investigator, February 2, 2014, https://quoteinvestigator.com/2012/05/26/stumble-over-truth.

5   Tom Osborne, *On Solid Ground* (Lincoln, NE: Nebraska Book, 1996), 21, 131–33.

6   Les Brown, *Live Your Dreams* (New York: William Morrow and Co., 1992), 75.

7   Gil Bailie, as quoted by John Eldredge, *Wild at Heart: Discovering the Secret of a Man's Soul* (Nashville, TN: Thomas Nelson, 2001), 200.

8   Angela L. Duckworth et al., "Cognitive and Noncognitive Predictors of Success," *Proceedings of the National Academy of Sciences of the United States of America* 116, no. 47 (November 4, 2019), 23499–504, https://www.pnas.org/content/116/47/23499. See also Ali Pattillo, "Study on Army Cadets Suggests 'Grit' Matters More Than Previously Thought," *Inverse*, November 4, 2019, https://www.inverse.com/article/60638-grit-may-be-the-key-to-success.

9   Thomas à Kempis, *The Imitation of Christ*, trans. E. M. Blaiklock (Nashville, TN: Thomas Nelson, 1979), bk. 2, chap. 12, para. 4.

10   John Barton, "The Golf Digest Interview: Condoleeza Rice," *Golf Digest*, May 1, 2011, https://www.golfdigest.com/story/condoleeza-rice-interview.

11   Julie Ray, "Nearly One in Four Worldwide Thriving," Gallup, April 10, 2012, http://www.gallup.com/poll/153818/Nearly-One-Four-Worldwide-Thriving.aspx?utm_source=alert&utm_medium=email&utm_campaign=syndication&utm_content=morelink&utm_term=All Gallup.

12   Anthony M. Daniels and J. Allister Vale, "Did Sir Winston Churchill Suffer from the 'Black Dog'?," *Journal of the Royal Society of Medicine* 111, no. 11 (October 2018), https://journals.sagepub.com/doi/full/10.1177/0141076818808428.

13   M. L. Cavanaugh, PhD, is a nonresident fellow with the Modern War Institute at West Point. His article is "Why America Needs Optimistic Generals," Modern War Institute, September 6, 2018, https://mwi.usma.edu/america-needs-optimistic-generals. He shows how optimism as a critical trait

among generals can compel their subordinates to give of their best while yet still burdened by doubts, despair, or pessimism for their cause.

14 See Zalman Nelson, "Never Quite Good Enough: Unrelenting Standards Life Pattern," blog, July 21, 2020, https://www.zalmannelson.com/post/2017/02/15/never-quite-good-enough-unrelenting-standards-life-pattern.

15 What follows was partly inspired by an article by Margarita Tartakovsky, "How to Relinquish Unrealistic Expectations," PsychCentral, May 17, 2016, https://psychcentral.com/lib/how-to-relinquish-unrealistic-expectations#1.

16 Jessica Stillman, "A 70-Year Study of 70,000 Children Says This Is the Secret to Raising Successful Kids," Inc.com, October 3, 2018, https://www.inc.com/jessica-stillman/scientists-followed-thousands-of-kids-for-70-years-this-is-biggest-takeaway-for-parents.html.

17 Seph Fontane Pennock, "The Hednoic Treadmill—Are We Forever Chasing Rainbows?," PositivePsychology.com, March 29, 2022, https://positivepsychology.com/hedonic-treadmill.

18 See Tartakovsky, "How to Relinquish Unrealistic Expectations."

19 For a fighter pilot to later refer to this coin as a "coin" is interpreted among fellow pilots as a challenge—a challenge that requires other fighter pilots to show that they have their coin on their person, a coin engraved with their call sign and gun number. Failure to show the RMO (round metal object) means that person must purchase a round of drinks for all thusly challenged. There are many other prohibited words and activities that are sacraments of a different sort.

20 Jim Mattis and Bing West, *Call Sign Chaos: Learning to Lead* (New York: Random House, 2019).

21 For example, see Ken Blanchard and Sheldon Bowles, *Raving Fans: A Revolutionary Approach to Customer Service* (New York: William Morrow and Co., 1993), and Ken Blanchard, *Leading at a Higher Level*, 3rd ed. (Hoboken, NJ: Pearson Education, 2019).

22 Robin Olds with Christina Olds and Ed Rasimus, *Fighter Pilot: The Memoirs of Legendary Ace Robin Olds* (New York: St. Martin's Press, 2010), 284.

23 Jim Collins, *Good to Great: Why Some Companies Make the Leap . . . and Others Don't* (New York: HarperCollins, 2001), 72.

24 My appreciation and credit to Mark Foreman, lead pastor at North Coast Calvary Chapel in Carlsbad, California, for his teaching and insights that informed this chapter.

25 The maverick missile has a large coupling that connects the electrical signals from the pilot controls in the cockpit to the missile. When the missile is fired, those signals are transmitted through the coupling and the missile launches, leaving the coupling still attached to the aircraft. So this coupling (or plug) becomes a great souvenir from a fired maverick missile for the crew chief.

26 This material is adapted from *Brain-Based Therapy with Adults: Evidence-Based Treatment for Everyday Practice*, by John B. Arden and Lloyd Linford (Hoboken, NJ: John Wiley & Sons, 2009).

27 Claudia P. Orlas et al., "Perceived Social Support Is Strongly Associated with Recovery after Injury," *Journal of Trauma and Acute Care Surgery* 91, no. 3 (September 2021): 552–58, https://journals.lww.com/jtrauma/Abstract/2021/09000/Perceived_social_support_is_strongly_associated.15.aspx; J. A. Kulik and H. I. Mahler, "Social Support and Recovery from Surgery," *Health Psychology* 8, no. 2, 221–38, https://pubmed.ncbi.nlm.nih.gov/2786808; Espen Andreas Brembo et al., "Role of Self-Efficacy and Social Support in Short-Term Recovery after Total Hip Replacement: A Prospective Cohort Study," *Health and Quality of Life Outcomes* 15, no. 68 (2017), https://doi.org/10.1186/s12955-017-0649-1.

28 American Psychological Association, *Stress in America: Paying with Our Health*, February 4, 2015, https://www.apa.org/news/press/releases/stress/2014/stress-report.pdf; Ramsey Solutions, "Money, Marriage, and Communication," September 27, 2021, https://www.ramseysolutions.com/relationships/money-marriage-communication-research.

29 Nancy Bilyeau, "Do You Work Longer Hours Than a Medieval Peasant?," Medium, https://tudorscribe.medium.com/do-you-work-longer-hours-than-a-medieval-peasant-17a9efe92a20; Niall McCarthy, "How Often

Do U.S. Workers Experience Abuse and Harassment?," Statista, August 15, 2017, https://www.statista.com/chart/10693/how-often-do-us-workers-experience-abuse-harassment;. Martin Armstrong, "Stress Is Biggest Threat to Workplace Health," Statista, October 24, 2016, https://www.statista.com/chart/6177/stress-is-biggest-threat-to-workplace-health.

30 Ben Renner, "Modern Family: Average Parent Spends Just 5 Hours Face-To-Face with Their Kids per Week," Study Finds, January 25, 2020, https://www.studyfinds.org/modern-family-average-parent-spends-just-5-hours-face-to-face-with-their-kids-per-week; Esteban Ortiz-Ospina, "Are Parents Spending Less Time with Their Kids?," Our World in Data, December 14, 2020, https://ourworldindata.org/parents-time-with-kids; Ananda Stuart et al., "An Evaluation of the Quality of Parent-Child Interactions in Vulnerable Families That Are Followed by Child Protective Services: A Latent Profile Analysis," *Children (Basel, Switzerland)* 8, no. 10 (2021), https://doi.org/10.3390/children8100906.

31 B. Cryer, "Neutralizing Workplace Stress: The Physiology of Human Performance and Organizational Effectiveness," paper presented at the Psychological Disabilities in the Workplace conference held at The Centre for Professional Learning, Toronto, California, June 12, 1996. See also "Stress in the Workplace: Stats and Quotes," Human Nature at Work, https://humannatureatwork.com/article/serious; "UCL Study: Overtime 'Bad for Your Heart,'" UCL, May 12, 2010, https://www.ucl.ac.uk/news/2010/may/ucl-study-overtime-bad-your-heart; "Study Shows How Stress at Work Is Linked to Heart Disease," UCL, January 23, 2008, https://www.ucl.ac.uk/news/2008/jan/study-shows-how-stress-work-linked-heart-disease.

32 See, for example, Matthew 8:34–9:1; 15:13–14; 27:12–14; Luke 4:28–30; 23:8–9. In his book *When to Walk Away: Finding Freedom from Toxic People* (Grand Rapids, MI: Zondervan, 2019), Gary Thomas states, "Jesus walked away from others (or let others walk away from him) more than two dozen times in the four gospels" (p. 25).

33 "Studies Show a 40% Decline in Empathy among College Students," Twenty One Toys, accessed June 20, 2022, https://twentyonetoys.com/blogs/teaching-empathy/empathy-decline-college-students.

34 Eric Durr, "Worldwide Flu Outbreak Killed 45,000," U.S. Army, August 31, 2018, https://www.army.mil/article/210420/worldwide_flu_outbreak_killed_45000_american_soldiers_during_world_war_i; "Stock Market Crash of 1929," History.com, April 27, 2021, https://www.history.com/topics/great-depression/1929-stock-market-crash.

35 Mark Batterson, *If: Trading Your If Only Regrets for God's What If Possibilities* (Grand Rapids, MI: Baker Books, 2015), 160.

36 Lewis, *The Screwtape Letters*, letter 15, p. 75.

37 "Mel Gibson: Benjamin Martin," from *The Patriot*, directed by Roland Emmerich (Culver City, CA: Columbia Pictures, 2000), IMDb, accessed June 20, 2022, https://www.imdb.com/title/tt0187393/characters/nm0000154.

A free ebook edition is available with the purchase of this book.

To claim your free ebook edition:

1. Visit MorganJamesBOGO.com
2. Sign your name CLEARLY in the space
3. Complete the form and submit a photo of the entire copyright page
4. You or your friend can download the ebook to your preferred device

A **FREE** ebook edition is available for you or a friend with the purchase of this print book.

CLEARLY SIGN YOUR NAME ABOVE

Instructions to claim your free ebook edition:
1. Visit MorganJamesBOGO.com
2. Sign your name CLEARLY in the space above
3. Complete the form and submit a photo of this entire page
4. You or your friend can download the ebook to your preferred device

Print & Digital Together Forever.

| Snap a photo | Free ebook | Read anywhere |

CPSIA information can be obtained
at www.ICGtesting.com
Printed in the USA
JSHW011340111022
31547JS00001B/3